Vicky Weston grew up in Tanganyika and Kenya partially during the Mau Mau uprising. She is a watercolourist, with a love of the sea and nature. She lived in France for several years, travelling in winter in a motorhome through Spain and Portugal. She is now retired and lives in New Zealand.

AROUND THE NEXT CORNER

For Jan, who always wanted to see what was round the next bend.

Vicky Weston

AROUND THE NEXT CORNER

AUSTIN MACAULEY
PUBLISHERS LTD.

A CIP catalogue record for this title is available from the British Library.

ISBN 978 184963 546 2

www.austinmacauley.com

First Published (2013)
Austin Macauley Publishers Ltd.
25 Canada Square
Canary Wharf
London
E14 5LB

Printed and Bound in Great Britain

Books by the Same Author

The View From Here
978 184963 224 9
Published 2013

Austin Macauley Publishers Ltd

Chapter 1

Winter Wonderland

A freezing wind cut through our thin clothing as we rode a swift tide upriver. On either hand the banks unwound slowly from the icy mists, warehouses, factories, high rise flats, the brownish smoking surface of the river itself animated by an occasional lone tug hauling lighters laden with the capital's accumulated rubbish, or half empty trip boats carrying chilled tourists towards Greenwich.

It came as a relief to find the bascules of Tower Bridge looming from the fog, the lock entrance we sought nestled into a concrete slot spanned by a white wooden bridge alongside the grotesque tiered pile of the Tower Hotel.

Our lives were about to change dramatically and there was nothing we could do about it but bow to the inevitable.

Sometimes life can resemble a series of stopovers. Like passengers deprived of a plane in mid-journey we find ourselves forced into unaccustomed situations unwillingly and for prolonged periods; this was one of them.

London is Mecca for the tourist; to us it's somewhere to go when choices become limited, when the bank starts reminding us about breaches of exchange control regulations and despatching urgent missives demanding that more normal relations be resumed as soon as possible.

To people like ourselves St Katherine's Dock was a 'haven' in more ways than one, its waters and silent warehouses given over to yachts, Thames barges, a maritime museum: it had become a microcosmic retreat amid the surrounding macrocosm of the City of London.

Few people ever give it much thought even if they know about it, most were unaware of its existence. Now and then a passing double-decker bus might have given its passengers a brief glimpse over high brick walls to mystical spars and pennants floating against a backdrop of yellowed brick or a circular white pergola isolated on its finger of grass-covered quay beneath a reflective façade of office windows staring blindly down.

But if those passengers had alighted and explored a bit further they might have discovered a hidden life within, for there existed at that time a veritable floating village, its dwellings a multitude of boats large and small bobbing on the speckled dock waters, moreover a village with its own rules, its own picturesque and turbid inhabitants all existing in blissful seclusion and totally oblivious to the lunchtime hordes seeking salubrious spots to consume their sandwiches or designer wines, most of them looking as alien to us as we must have seemed to them.

All this lay in the future; for now it was enough to decide whether we could afford the first month's mooring fees, eat or wash clothes and ourselves ere our money ran out.

We were broke; five years in the sunshine of the Mediterranean had given us many things but not financial stability, we'd seen our overdraft creep up, our income creep down, the Pound floating and our boat slowly declining to do so, something had to give. After a lot of thought about possible alternatives – none of which seemed practicable any more – and a good bit of heart searching, we'd finally decided to take the first favourable wind and head back home to England.

San Antonio, Ibiza is a wonderful place to get away from, I can state this with certitude having spent ten nights anchored off its beach, enduring a 'Med' storm and learning the words of 'Viva Espana' and 'Una Paloma Blanca' endlessly chanted at full volume by that odd new phenomenon, the half inebriated office worker (of both sexes) which has turned a once lovely island paradise into a ghastly seedy disco.

Of course one ought not to generalise but that was how it seemed at the time.

We fled the moment the wind allowed us to do so; the new breeze was from the west, its direction and our empty purse dictated that we point our reluctant bowsprit towards the north and home once more.

Barcelona served us just long enough to refuel, then we were off and two days later eased the boat into the sheltering entrance of La Nouvelle at the head of the Golf de Lion, our journey now a matter of urgency before the canals froze over or sections were drained for out of season repairs.

A canal voyage in winter becomes a serious affair; gone are the sun-scalds and the gently flowing waters of summer, the leafy shaded aisles and sunbaked reaches of the outward journey where we had yearned for the cooler stretches as one yearns for water in the desert.

This is a harsher world by far with winter and hunger hammering on the door; a world of sudden storms, savage gusts, turbid waters, leaf-littered slippery surfaces, icy grasses, cold steaming breath and the exhaust smoke hanging heavy in our reluctant wake.

Frost sears miasmas from the water's surface, towpaths are wet and slick with icy puddles, ropes become stiff and brutal to numbed fingers, gloves get wet and can't be dried, there is need for haste for soon the northern canals will become icebound, making any movement impossible.

Further warnings of the lateness of our journey evidenced as we struggled across the river Aude whose flooded, flotsam-speckled waters thrust angrily at the hull and tried to drive us onto the weir. A grim half hour saw us finally in the safety of the further lock but it was a reminder that this would be a hard and unforgiving journey.

Days ran into each other, blankets of smoke from canal-side bonfires hung low over the water and lagoons were silent places peopled by moribund barges, animated only by the barking of a distant farm dog as the bright frost-laden sky spoke of increasing cold.

Toulouse: a silent city as we arrived, autumn leaves flecked its canals piling up under bank-side trees, the waters smoked in the dawns and deserted cafes were firmly shuttered as we crept back into the basin.

We stayed no longer than necessary to fuel up and buy a

few provisions with our dwindling cash before sliding under the tunnel leading to the Canal Lateral.

This passed in a blur of freezing nights and ice-rimed locks. We locked out at Castets onto a flooded river Garonne bearing massed clumps of detritus – tree trunks, branches, and half submerged carcases on its brown waters.

Wary of the swift flood waters we waited until dead slack water before essaying the brick bridge at Bordeaux, mindful of its duplicity, for it had tried to drown us on the journey south, and we tied up on the yacht club pontoon for just long enough to get the mast back up and ready ourselves for the passage to come. Our journey down the Gironde was swift but our hopes of making straight to sea were dashed by gales and we had to cower in the shelter of Port Bloc watching the ferry make its turbulent trips across to Royan and the town's comforts, going easily where we could not.

When we did sail it was into one of the biggest swells we had ever seen, a turmoil of tide and sea forced by a racing ebb tide which bore us inevitably outward with the 'Corduron' reef a raging maelstrom to be avoided and a large cargo boat coming in vanishing completely behind each wave as we surfed along.

Reaching La Roche Bernard a few days later after a hard slog up the coast against the north west winds, we anchored in the pool hard by the barrage. It seemed hard to recall the warm night we had spent moored just below the barrage on the trip south, watching small fishing boats weaving complex lamp-lit patterns around us as they hunted fish-lets penned against the rearing edifice by the flood tide five years ago. Now all was silent, uninviting and chill.

We stopped briefly at La Roche Bernard, hastening to get the gear down again; Duck hunters haunted the reed beds as we passed, and Redon was bleak and unwelcoming. Locking out into the river Villaine we discovered that it was in dramatic flood; its current nearly defeated us as, with engine thundering, we crept along between nebulous banks, their outlines indeterminate under seething ochre waters, a few fence posts protruding like palsied fingers, and we navigated largely by them and the bank-side bushes now half submerged.

It was a relief to get to Rennes and into the canal, but ice clinked and fragmented as the lock shut behind us and the waters had a thick unyielding look about them, it was, we felt, now or never!

Early morning fields were frosted, breath hung steaming and we were noticing our lack of suitable clothing very much; the years in the Med had done nothing for our wardrobes, and sailing boots worn without socks, or thin-worn sneakers were insufficient for coping with frozen towpaths and lock margins.

Some mornings we found that we were shunting ice outside locks until the sun rose; gates were hard to open properly, and small floes washed out with us from each lock, we seemed to be the only thing moving, and heads were shaken by some, 'Chomages' were overdue and they thought we might get caught, fortunately we spoke to a lockkeeper who assured us that he would personally telephone ahead and make sure the system stayed open a couple more days, He was as good as his word, and our passage was uninterrupted.

In St Malo we spent a brief couple of days while we rigged for sea, Jan flew back to England leaving me to get the boat home and by waiting on the weather by dint of hard sailing and a brief stopover in Guernsey I got the boat back to England.

The 'dream' was faded, its shine almost gone, for now we couldn't see far enough ahead to know when or whether there would be another 'corner to look round' let alone a new dream we might cling to...

Chapter 2

Recovery

Over the next few years we did hold onto the dream though it often faded badly. We grew to know our small world and its characters, its stresses, its impermanence and challenges: those weeks when it was a choice between eating or paying the mooring fees, when a trip to the supermarket meant juggling pennies and leaving something behind if our sums hadn't worked out.

Friends inviting one for a meal meant an easier week, returning the favour meant going without, for all of us at that time were financially challenged yet somehow we got through; the acquaintances of those days became firm friends, the people we could rely on if things got tough, Some of them still are...adversity brings understanding. Nearly everyone in St Katherine's was a financial or social refugee, or had a project going which necessitated their staying in the capital to earn money. Wages were high compared to other places, options wide: you could almost always get a job, at weekends many did, and we could take comfort that we need not drive out to the countryside to find leisure; a lively social life existed based on shared poverty, we sat around on each others' decks or cabins. Occasionally someone bought in a bottle of good wine, mostly it was plonk, it reminded me very forcefully of John Steinbeck's 'Cannery Row' with the bums sitting out on the porch drinking from old fruit jars, at least, that's how it felt and we didn't care because at the time there was nothing to care about.

St Katherine's was full of 'characters', many owned boats, some didn't and there existed a fringe of 'come and go' pop-up figures from around the local community who made use of the 'yacht club' from time to time and who we grew to know rather well. Convenient to the City and East End it had become a haven for social refugee and seedy villain alike, a watering spot for one or two of the East End's less salubrious inhabitants, where one could discover almost every aspect of the human condition, and often did!

It was not uncommon to play darts with a small time villain or to share a drink with a 'minder' or see deals going down which, in a gentler place one might have considered reprehensible.

Such things as cannabis drew no remark, it circulated freely around Dock and nearer environs. To visit one or two of the barges was to be enveloped in a miasma of fumes, most of which would leave you light-headed, indeed one poor fellow who worked with Customs had learned to develop a selective sense of smell; his life would have been unbearable had he noticed half of what went on in any official capacity... Sensibly he kept his council and his thoughts to himself, preserving both his anonymity and his friends.

We found out these things gradually; the permanent residents tended to be clannish at first, assessing you before opening up and sharing their knowledge and experience, The core group consisted of the owners and crews of the several Thames sailing barges which were based in the dock: these were of varying kinds, some of them company-owned or craft linked to a riverside business where, by 'tradition', much of their production over the years had been transported in fleets of barges: cement, bricks, brewery products, and a myriad more goods were transported by these elegant vessels, and as they went into decline with the increase in the use of road transport and railways, so were the vessels broken up, some wrecked, others dragooned into war service and many were lost. Yet others went over to Dunkirk and helped bring home weary troops, or carried supplies to the beaches, their flat bottoms making them ideal for this work; many of these were sunk by mine, bomb, artillery fire, or storm, and those that came home often succumbed to neglect and eventual decay.

Now here in the dock were some of the few remaining vessels still afloat, some under company flag, others privately owned and cared for and on several occasions throughout the year, raced against others of their kind.

Some old salts still sailed in them and these shellbacks enlivened many an evening in the club or get-togethers aboard each other's craft, regaling their listeners with stories of the days when the barges had traded, tales recounted in broad Suffolk idioms entertaining, redolent with nostalgic yearnings for older ways and times.

Anyone owning their own barge had to be eccentric it went with the job! Keeping them running called for cunning and ingenuity, a deep pocket or compensating skills in many trades; nothing less was qualification to run a barge successfully.

It was hardly surprising therefore to find among the owners: lawyers, semi drop-outs, enthusiastic amateurs, skilled professionals, and a motley collection of 'hangers-on' who tended the needs of their huge charges with all the dedication of stable grooms, and who were available to help crew the big barges when they raced.

In their working days it was said they could be, and often were, run by just a man and a boy, or skipper and mate combination. Many of the stories revolved around being short-handed in heavy weather, and working the barge, loading and unloading, cleaning the holds ready for the next cargo and sailing the barge to her next port, river, creek or wharf, often up narrow isolated waterways to remote jetties serving small communities. When it is realised that these barges were often eighty feet or more in length and weighed in at around seventy tons and more, the skills involved in sailing and running them can be easily appreciated.

Rigged for ease of handling yet they still carried the great topsails which could be set high on the long topmast to catch wayward airs in narrow creeks or built-up dock areas, and whether sailing towing or warping around crowded docks and waterways. the level of skill displayed was often astonishing, even among their latter-day amateur owners.

A barge often took the ground at low tide settling on 'camp sheds' – specially raised and levelled areas along the river wharves where they could take the ground safely – yet even here the strains on their hulls as they dried out sometimes provoked odd behaviours, such as internal doors not shutting until the vessel floated again. Occasionally they got stuck down in the mud on poorly maintained berths when the tide rose again and the apocryphal tale was of the mate being sent up to the masthead with a hammer to smite the spars top, the vibrations this caused, it was said, broke the suction and the barge floated again, though I never saw it done.

Now the occasional rare freight had given way to leisure use, hiring out to parties as venues for city company meetings or lunches, and owners eked a living where they could.

Several kept their barge in the dock as a convenient pied a terre during the week; for some of them the boat was their only home.

In a world where property prices in central London were beginning to go through the proverbial roof, a boat was an affordable option, convenience could be a strong factor, many like ourselves worked around the City and St Katherine's was an ideal haven.

Its centre for us was Beth's shop, she wasn't the owner, but from her vantage point behind the plate glass fronting onto the footbridge and club quay, she missed little of what went on.

If we wanted to know each other's whereabouts at any time we'd pop in and ask: there would almost always be a satellite trail of boaties or locals chatting to Beth, it was our gossip exchange, refuge, parliament, and occasional provider of gifts.

In times of want one could nearly always find a fag, a potential meal, help when wanted, crew, or a social partner for an event, Beth provided them all in one way or other.

If she did not know about something, she would find out, her Yellow Pages was greasy and well-thumbed, her cigarettes freely shared, she was indispensable...

Canny with the wisdom and humour of her Welsh ancestry, she could always be relied upon for a joke, a smile, a strong shoulder to cry on, a ready encourager when things got a bit glum.

She was unpartisan with her favour, indispensable as a favourite teddy bear, and had a wise and wicked humour that saw us through many a crisis; life would have been infinitely poorer without her.

A busy sub-culture ran beneath the outward appearance of the dock based around a mutual reliance; it saw craftsmen engaged in maintaining the boats and gear. Several plied their trade freely; one could often find riggers and shipwrights, painters and caulkers available through the gossip exchange, to undertake almost any job.

We had in addition a hairdresser, a grocery store, yacht agents and the club, while the Tower Hotel itself provided employment and occasional rooms for guests, particularly if ongoing repairs meant that barge accommodation was unavailable or one had visitors unaccustomed to boat living.

All of this contributed to the internal economy of the place, and most of the inhabitants spent much of their income in the local shop, only going outside to a supermarket or laundromat when necessary. Even the yachts and barges were serviced, in that around the area several chandlers plied their trade, and an old fashioned ship chandler lay just a few blocks away, where vessels could find the kind of gear needed to keep them running. One of its delights was the scents in their dingy premises, smells of tar and hemp, ironwork, sisal and coiled rope and cordage.

Elderly gnomes in brown overalls took your order before vanishing into the back regions delving knowledgably amongst their stock to find the particular item one wanted.

Occasionally one would be invited in there to look for particular things, and it was always a joy to search among sacks of rope, shelves of galvanized rigging-screws, shackles, bolts, gunny sacks of copper fastenings, oakum and caulking cotton, and fingering marlin spikes and caulking irons, mallets or tins of marine glue.

These Aladdin's caves always delighted me, and still do, though they have largely disappeared along with so much else in favour of modern chrome and glass emporia aseptic and charmless.

Slowly by dint of living carefully, working hard and saving up we began to dig ourselves out of our self-created financial hole resuming a fairly normal life, nothing dramatic just steady and solid; the nasty tasting medicine was beginning to work...!

At times when the close environs of the place palled, we would leave the Dock's comforts to sail down to Sheerness. The Thames is not an easy river for sailing craft, swift tides create many problems: local currents can turn direction within a few dozen yards, trots of moored lighters make for obstacles requiring skill and confidence to negotiate safely, in addition the river twists and writhes like an eel as it pursues its course between banks cluttered here by small quays, jetties, warehouses businesses and yards.

To yachts such as ourselves the Thames presents a challenge, for at every turn one finds the wind shut off or diverted by buildings into all kinds of odd gusts, slants and calms. Negotiating it requires alertness and courage, and a good eye to seek out places where an adverse current may suddenly sweep you helpless onto moored lighters with devastating results.

Yet the trip had its charms, you saw London through its backdoor; you saw its development and growth in the patterns of shed and ancient shipyard. Beneath your feet great tunnels carried the daily warp and weft of urgent traffic, and further down you encountered its architectural heritage as the noble buildings of Greenwich are passed, with Brunel's pedestrian tunnel deep below your keel.

Dock entrances tell of a past when the river was in full and frantic daily use. History was made here, and indeed, it was from one of these that our family set out on its first voyage to Africa, as will be related.

Meanwhile the new line of the Thames Barrier lay across one's track, its multi-towers punctuating its length, the passage no great problem unless a spring tide should be racing through the gaps, especially on the ebb, making the passage laborious and difficult to low-powered vessels such as ourselves.

Standing between London and its inundation by hundred-year floods this vast project is supposed to manage all but extreme conditions, those of us around in the 50s recall only too well how extreme some of those conditions can be…!

The barrier, it's said, will prevent this happening but I for one have doubts. Mother Nature has shown herself quite capable of overcoming any man-made obstacle under the right conditions, but as you sail past it's probably better to look on the bright side and be grateful that it provides at least some reassurance for London's citizenry.

Beyond, one is flanked by power stations, new town type housing, the Thames unreels before you, bend following bend, until the sewage depot and its attendant satellites – the 'Bovril boats' as the sludge tankers are known – tell you that the Royal docks have been passed, and you are on the way to wider and less populated waters.

Beckton power station slides astern and here the river broadens, giving the sailor more space for longer tacks against the wind, or sometimes 'slashing' voyages with the wind blowing clear across the marshes giving one pleasure in sailing the boat rather than worrying about errant currents and obstacles.

Sheets are taut, the wind strong and only as you approach Gravesend does the river narrow again with its jetties, moored craft and ferry traffic. Threading a course through it all one passes Gravesend itself, the customs jetty and the port authority, the moored 'Sun' tugs awaiting business, and then shortly the squat outlines of the Gravesend forts dominate the left bank as it curves away into the distance and you find yourself negotiating a wide bend where very often a short sea gets chopped up by wind over tide, or the wash coming up Sea reach. Pass Mucking flats and the oil terminals and you may have an easy sail onward or a hard, chilly and bitter battle against tide wind and waves to reach the comparative peace of the lee by the Isle of Sheppey.

Our destination was often a night at anchor in one of the silent creeks of the Medway as the tide turned against us, making it an ideal destination, it was 'our' time for relaxation leaving the frustrations of the City behind us and allowing the peace of the waterways to seep over us.

But these trips could also produce moments of humour: friends came with us one weekend, enjoying the trip down to a quiet anchorage just outside the fairway close to the marsh edge.

At two o'clock in the morning we heard a scream: investigating we discovered Chrissy sitting up in bed clutching her covers around her and staring petrified at the floor where the ship's cat and a large rat were facing off aggressively. By luck I was able to grab the rodent by its long tail and hurl it through the nearest porthole into the river much to the cat's disgust; clearly she had caught it somewhere in the dock area and bringing it aboard, had lost it down the bilges, only now had she rediscovered it. Chrissy was calmed, the cat chided, and we all went back to bed.

Sophie the cat had other little habits, she liked to sneak aboard neighbouring boats and steal food from them. On one occasion she returned with a fillet of beef, on another, half a cooked chicken, we never dared ask around who might have lost things in this way; fortunately she was never caught in the act.

One day sailing down channel off Ramsgate, she decided to jump overboard and swim to Belgium... I had to heave to, launch the dinghy, and paddle off to rescue the crazy creature who was happily on her way to Ostend, while the yacht heaved and swayed drunkenly on the swells, clearly Sophie had no idea of fear.

A few weeks later she disappeared for over a month. We feared her drowned, for she had a habit of standing up on her hind legs to swat flies on the foredeck and its rail was open at that point; perhaps she overbalanced, usually when she fell in she got out by means of the rope fenders we kept dangling for her. This time there was no sign of her until a month later when she arrived back stick thin, evidently having been very ill. The vet said he thought she had fallen into an oil slick and swallowed quite a lot before crawling to somewhere she could hide, to die or recover. Her throat had been burned by what she had swallowed. But she survived, and stayed with us for another six months ere she had to leave us.

Eventually she was found a country home living in a big caravan near Maidenhead along with four other cats and an adoring new owner. We were told later that she immediately took over and ruled the roost for many years.

Life on the water has other compensations, its characters and the friends met, together with a shifting and brotherly camaraderie that takes over wherever you go; you may anchor in a creek behind another yacht or barge, and often you will know or get to know its crew, or find you have friends in common.

In addition there is something very special in sharing these occasions: some of our happiest days have been spent anchored in a river or creek with a couple of good pals, yarning, eating. racing each others' dinghies, swimming and enjoying the simple fact of each other's company... often amid a silence that can be felt, as tidal waters fret the boat's hull and redshanks and gulls mew along the tide's edge, there is the sound of a distant church bell, the rattle of pans from the galley, and the chink of filled glasses; such times are worth more than gold.

Getting back to base in the dock could be exciting if the wind had got up or changed direction overnight, surging up-river under shortened canvas enjoying a slashing sail but with one eye very firmly on the Locks' opening times, for if you miss the tide, you have to spend a night out on the river pontoon which is bumpy from passing ferry traffic.

In winter it was sometimes hard living aboard, we installed a small wood burning stove, and this kept the cabin fairly warm but there were many mornings when the dock would be slick with ice, even snow on one occasion, and once we had a real freeze-up lasting several days, clearly we should have to think hard about living aboard in England, as a longer term solution.

There were times when we would have to lower the boat's tall mast in order to take a trip upriver, for the Thames bridges were far too low for us to pass with it up. This usually happened so that we might put the boat onto a hard and attend to the marine growths on her bottom; this also involved repainting the bottom afterwards to protect her against barnacles and borers.

We were fortunate in having a boat whose hull had been sheathed in glass fibre when she was built. This had been done in South Africa, and much of her construction was of African hardwoods. We knew that the gales she had encountered had thoroughly tested her on the voyage back to England.

Still, the unpleasant job had to be done every year or so, and we would lock out onto the first of a flood tide and carry it upriver to Brentford, near which was a solid gravel bank alongside a quay which was not only a pleasant location but handy to a pub. There, if we had timed things right we could go alongside and, as the tide fell, dry out comfortably more or less on a level and with a good gravel bottom to keep us clean while we repainted.

As the waters fell we would begin by scrubbing and cutting away the accumulated growths from the hull, using sharp hoes and washing off with river water, then as the boat dried out and the hull became accessible we would begin repainting.

It could be a congenial task. Friends were often inveigled with promises of liquid refreshments and a picnic lunch to come and spend a damp hour or two under the boat slapping antifouling paint on the boat's bottom and on themselves, discovering as they painted that doing so above your head can lead to the paint running down your arms and getting into your hair as you struggle to move yourself along her length while squashed into a space just over two feet deep, comments were often interesting...

Well-wishers too cheered or jeered from the quay above, or could be persuaded into fetching refreshing cold drinks and sandwiches from the pub; all in all it was always a very happy few hours until the tide rose again.

Job done, we would occasionally slip through the sea lock and up to Twickenham to see friends who owned a boatyard nearby.

One day, having a bank holiday weekend and a delayed

chance at slipping the boat for repairs, we decided to take her through the back reaches of London via the Regent's Canal, emerging eventually down at Limehouse Basin before going back upriver for our appointment.

It proved a voyage of discovery in more ways than one: our first excitement was a 'flasher' on the opposite bank who seemed to think an airing might help his tan, frankly we'd seen better things dead on sticky fly paper, and told him so at which he hastily recovered himself and rode off red-faced.

Next we had a brief encounter with an armchair seat wrapping round the propeller. This, as has been said elsewhere is becoming a common experience; canals seem to attract domestic rubbish in large quantities, and this took a huge effort waist-deep in filthy water to cut it free, luckily we had invested in some seriously tough cutters for just such emergencies and eventually were able to chop our way through its hardened springs and free ourselves.

Travelling as it does through London's back door one is permanently entertained by the variety and sometimes beauty of some of the canal-side gardens, while areas such as Paddington Basin and the attractive environs of Little Venice hint at an ongoing leisure usage of these old waterways which helps to preserve a bit of the magic that parts of London have to offer the persistent tourist.

Passing through Marylebone, an area we both knew well, was both charming and instructive, it made us realise how superficial was our normal contact with its busy streets. Here lay another and hidden world, its gardens almost a part of the waterway, aged industries' footprints still large among them, Steptoe-scrapyards, warehouses, car dumps and then the sudden and startling transition to Regent's Park and the Zoo following our open-mouthed and extraordinary journey among the exhibits with tourist boats plying a busy trade around us before we reached the bustle of Hampstead Road lock and the vibrancy of a crowded Camden Market in full swing nearby.

Here we had our second alien encounter as an enthusiastic 'streaker' dived naked into the cut and swam desperately after us to the encouraging cheers of an interested audience. In those days phone cameras were not invented, so his exposure was less than he might have hoped for in these less inhibited times but it did provide some more amusement to enliven our journey, and here we found many who were fascinated to see our boat in such an unlikely setting, so we tied up and chatted for a while.

The canal from here on began to look both bleak and commercial as we travelled, tall brick warehouse and factory walls gave space to dim and silent backwaters or 'cuts' mysterious and silent reminding one of Fagin's backyard in the film Oliver, all green weed, mud and dereliction, old rotting gantries protruding from upper-storey loading platforms, ready gibbets for an erring pickpocket or cutpurse...

Kings Cross and St Pancras led us towards Islington tunnel where a dark slit vanished into stygian gloom, with a faint blob of ethereal light just visible at its far end; it was an eerie place and we were relieved on emerging to find the sun still shining despite appearances!

We finally spent the night moored beside Victoria Park, around us the vibrant throb of the metropolis, overhead a basket of jewelled stars despite the glow of distant lighting, the stealthy meanderings and exploring of a few stray cats and what could have been a rat in a nearby rubbish bin. London dozed its way towards a misty dawn, when all the bustle would begin again.

Jan was tempted to make a quick foray home for a forgotten book, but we decided that the risk was not worth the effort – she might easily have been unable to get out of the park at that time of night, never mind the chances of finding her way back in.

The following morning after a misty start, we essayed the last pram and litter-peppered reaches to emerge at length from the last lock into the wide basin at Limehouse, deserted now, its trade all but moribund. A Dutch coaster loaded scrap metal from a rusting pile on one quay and a few decaying boats told the tale of slow abandonment and dereliction encroaching on so many of these smaller dock areas, uneconomic now, frequented by occasional vessels.

But there is renewal, Slowly a new phenomenon is happening, the buying and conversion of old warehouse facilities into designer 'pied a terres' bought by an increasingly affluent class of City whiz kids, to whom a bijou riverfront residence is swiftly becoming the 'must have' of the eighties, There is new hope, a new chapter beginning: soon we won't know the place!

We locked out into the river again through a huge gate and a vast chamber in which we were the only craft. Somehow the tidal river seemed very welcoming as we made our way back upstream once more, our suspended appointment with the boatyard now poised for the following day.

Followed three weeks of hard and unpleasant work, the fibreglass sheathing along each angle of the hull was cracking badly letting water in, our boat was what is known as 'hard chined', that's to say she had a hull which had sharp corners below the waterline, where sides and bottom met, the whole covered in fibreglass layers and despite being gently eased by a narrow rounded area, these were now splitting along their length where the resin was failing, and needed to be cut back to sound material, dried out thoroughly and then ground down and tapered to form a fillet to which the new fibreglass could be bedded.

Glassfibre is a wonderful material as long as you never have to touch it, but start to sand it and a storm of tiny splinters get everywhere and when they touch skin they itch. No matter how careful we were in wrapping towels around our necks and wearing breathing masks while we worked, by day's end we would be driven almost insane by the irritation, it came as a relief when at last the sanding and grinding were done and we could begin to rebuild the glass sheathing layer by layer until once again it was as thick and sound as the original.

What made the job bearable was that after work we could shower and slip away house-hunting around the area, and thus we found our Twickenham home.

At this time Margaret Thatcher the new Prime Minister had begun to put in place her own dream, that of seeing people owning and upgrading their own homes; all at once the GLC began to give one hundred per cent mortgages to help people buy council flats and to update some of its ailing properties around the London area, so with eyes set on the future, we were not slow in applying.

Our first purchase had been a grotty ground floor flatlet, part of a 'Peabody' block in a run-down area of Bethnal Green in Pritchard's Road and despite being opposite the Pimms factory, did well for us. The area had a bad reputation for crime, break-ins in the block being commonplace but we managed to do the flat up to a good standard, avoid being robbed of too much, and were able to sell it on profitably within a couple of years. Our trips upriver meanwhile, had convinced us that Twickenham and Teddington held much promise for the future.

Once the Bethnal green flat had sold we replaced it quickly with a vertical 'salt and pepperbox' Victorian house just behind the main street in Twickenham, backing onto a Chinese takeaway at the front and a rubber factory at the back. Despite these olfactory disadvantages we liked it and saw its potential; over the next couple of years we converted its upper story into a tasteful small flat, updated the property with an inside bathroom and new kitchen, put in gas, water and central heating and revamped the exterior.

The roof was retiled again courtesy of the 'improvement loans scheme' of the time and together with our neighbours, a very pleasant ex-student foursome, we worked up the gardens, put in paving and sheds, new fences and plantings and acquired a lodger.

He came to us on a trial basis of a month and stayed eight years; he moved with us as part of the furniture, he was the perfect foil for our spats, a wonderful tenant and a house-wife's dream.

If anything wanted doing we had only to mention it and it would be done: he washed up, walked our dog, fetched and carried for Jan's elderly Mum, and if we could have cloned him we'd have made a fortune.

Every home should have one! To our lasting joy and regret

he met a lovely lady and married her, our loss was her gain, and our good wishes for their happiness were heartfelt.

We now had our feet firmly planted on the property ladder, and at last could look to a new future.

Life on the boat was coming to an end anyhow. Authority had stepped in and shortly 'live-aboards' would be banned permanently they suggested, it was the writing on the wall. Civilization was rapidly setting its claws into freedoms of all sorts and this was just another such example.

Three years on we sold the Twickenham home for what seemed an unreasonably high sum and bought an Edwardian house on the edge of Teddington's high street. It was an uninspiring start, someone had painted it black all over on the outside, red and green inside and it took us a couple of years to put everything right, the way we wanted it, with modest light mushroom exterior, creamy interior walls complementing the stripped pine doors, and an elegant white stairway to the upper floor.

We also re-did the kitchen, lined the loft, installed a new bathroom, and generally made the place saleable as well as attractive.

Once again the Gods blessed their errant children by allowing Jan to foresee the '87 housing crash. We got clear of the property against all advice and market belief just in time, completing its sale three weeks before the implosion which left many unlucky house owners so badly stranded.

Meanwhile we had begun to travel once more, the spark and our dream were still alive. We had recharged ourselves financially, and reaching out we could catch the dream again in mid-flight...

Chapter 3

The Ruined Barn

We had never forgotten our first dalliance with France, and when the time came for a holiday we accepted the invitation of a couple of St Katherine's friends to go down to their new home in the Dordogne.

Together over the years of friendship we'd often discussed buying property over there, stimulated by adverts in a paper, and faded pictures of exciting looking properties, all it seemed, at ridiculously low prices. At that time you could purchase a home in France for around twenty thousand pounds, which was amazingly cheap by English standards. They'd finally taken the plunge and bought a lovely old home on the side of a hill near Les Ezyies de Tayac in the Dordogne region, pictures they sent us showed a rambling confection of bakery, barn, terrace and main dwelling clustered around a large raised courtyard and with a drive of creamy gravel and a couple of acres, part woodland, part field.

Wild boar tenanted their small copse and ran riot through their lawns at night, doing a much better job than any tractor as they searched out acorns and truffles.

Together with 'Spike' their fox terrier and 'Scoop' a longhaired sheepdog, they seemed to have landed in paradise and we took up their invitation to spend some time with them, eagerly. The drive down was long, and we almost got wiped out in the last ten minutes due to forgetting which side of the country lane we were supposed to be on, but we finally arrived, had tea, and rested awhile before supper, and our very first night saw us dining al fresco beneath a burgeoning grapevine under a vast and open sky, marvelling at dozens of fireflies flitting among the bushes, while we drank in the comforting scents and sights of a place far away from cities and pollution. The night was aglow with scintillating stars, the

Milky Way a great band of amorphous light, amid a silence that was absolute. Never had we seen so many new worlds, it was like touching on a vision for the first time, awe-inspiring and wonderful, in that evening we were finally hooked on France.

Our own experiences had also nudged us towards her, the love affair had begun when, as young dreamers, we had taken our small yacht down through the western canal system and in a short space of time, learned to love the country and its peoples, its changing landscapes, its waterside villages and tiny hilltop towns, its culture and cuisine, but above all the sense of space beginning to be so threatened back at home by thoughtless development and gradual erosions of the green belt.

France still retained enough space to find kilometre after kilometre of deserted roads, woodlands, open fields, areas of 'bocage' and river bottom land, rivers that still ran clear and unpolluted, and a sense of homecoming which we found hard to resist.

Our friends had settled most contentedly into their new house and it was not long before we felt as they did, as if we'd always been here and always would. Our love affair was confirmed and by the following day we too had made an offer on a property.

Quite how one can go for coffee and croissants at ten in the morning and by late afternoon have made an offer on a semi-derelict barn still bemuses me, but that's exactly what we did...

First impressions: an overgrown and decidedly damp walk up half a mile of trackway terminated in a glimpse among the trees of a creamy-grey building with another tree growing through its roof and brambles and nettles forming a tight barrier around its feet. Shattered tiles crunched underfoot as we drew nearer, the estate 'agent' exhorting us to beware of vipers which it seemed, might be lurking in the thick grasses.

Closer inspection was encouraging; a great peace hung over the land, a wood of acacia and oak lay to one side of the property, whilst a long and overgrown track might easily form a future driveway; the tree through the roof was largely moribund and easily disposed of and just at that moment the sound of a church bell came clear across the intervening woodland serving to remind us that the village was but a short walk away and necessities of life readily available if one chose to live here in this tranquil spot.

We explored, forcing open the great faded doors with their deliciously curved tops and nailed-plank construction revealing inside piles of straw together with an unpleasant amount of decaying manure at one end, and with an acrid ammonia smell. But rustic chestnut hay racks lined the walls, there was part of a cement floor, while vast quantities of sisal string depended in mad tangles from rusting nails or protruded through the gaping woodworm-infested boards of an upper level; the beams supporting this were simple rough cut tree trunks liberally studded with nails, bit of old iron, leather harness, more string and rusting wire.

But it was cool, one could see even now how it might make a comfortable and unique home given love and a lot of work and at the asking price, a mere ten thousand pounds sterling, it was a bargain!

True this would be raised by tax, agent's fees, notaire, and 'geometre' fees, but even so we felt that with a bit of creativity and after our experiences in the UK, it was something we might throw our effort into without reserve...

It was easy to forget that it lay ten hours south of the English Channel, that the land around it would require constant clearing every time we came down, that language was going to be a problem for quite a while and for the moment at least, you're going to have to slum it!

Fortunately our years of boating had made us adept at living in small spaces and with very little comfort so we were only mildly concerned by the lack of amenities...

But then dreams are never very strong on reality and by evening we had gone ahead and put in our offer anyway... which was accepted with a promptness which might have seemed suspicious in other circumstances.

Doing up a foreign property at a distance isn't always a

good idea however appealing it may seem at the time. Language leaves a lot of room for misunderstanding, the absentee owner gets put to the back of the builder's queue only to be resurrected if that individual suddenly finds himself short of a job.

When we bought there was a rising tide of prosperity among the tradespeople largely due to the influx of foreigners and local initiatives to create unsightly but affordable housing on small estates on the edge of villages, and we suffered the consequences in things promised but not done, or occasional slapdash work, though blessedly most of the local craftsmen were good at their trade, and even managed by means of gestures and stick drawings in the earth outside, to understand our needs and convey their own suggestions; mankind would have been the poorer without mother earth's own blackboard, as civilizations evolved!

But we made our mistakes too...

One of them was through trying to short circuit the local labour problems by getting 'ex pats' to do some of the jobs; such newcomers were always looking and advertising for work and foolishly we entrusted an early task to one such outfit.

We had been fortunate to begin with, in finding a very good artisan locally who had re-roofed the barn sympathetically, using the 'tuille platte' of its original covering together with some aged replacements which blended perfectly and gave it an original wavy and old look.

Once covered and weatherproofed we could begin clearing out the interior and we descended on our new home one holiday over a three week period and got to work. The string was fairly easy even if tangled, and the pile of old flooring lying in a corner only needed moving, we easily took down the partitions for the animals, but we had completely underestimated the dung.

It had been lying here added to by successive generations of cattle for many years, clearly the theory had been that if you wanted your animals to spend warm winters you simply ignored the deepening layers and welcomed each new addition.

Now however the summer's heat had baked it dry, or so

we fondly imagined. The first blow from our mattock revealed an appalling truth the stuff, far from being solid was very much like a peat bog: a layer of crust on top and below it a soggy quagmire, smelly, indescribably hard to shovel, a claggy mass tapering front to back over a metre deep at the rear and there were literally tons of it!

First thoughts of spreading some to create a vegetable garden faded as the sheer scale of the job impinged upon our befuddled minds; desperately we fought fatigue and flies, chopping it into barrow-sized chunks and tottering along narrow planks to where we could dump it away from the barn itself before struggling back for another load, it took nearly a week just to get to the bottom of it, the smell and residues of our efforts were with us for many weeks afterwards, and had still not faded by the time we had our next holiday.

Lesson: suggest to previous owners that *they* remove such impediments for you, and preferably a good while before you arrive…

We knew exactly what we wanted but getting it proved a lot harder than we had thought. A local builder undertook to excavate the floor and lay concrete over layers of plastic sheet and insulation, promising a sound job without problems. In the process of his labours we learned several more lessons.

First, don't go away while important things like this are being done; stay until the work is complete, haunt the site until it is.

Agree what you expect and want done beforehand, together with outlines of remedial action to be taken if things don't go according to plan, not just what you want now, but also covering future difficulties.

Because we neglected to do and say these things we lost the whole rear wall in a pile of rubble and dust when the builder began to excavate, I had had suspicions about it but the builder with panache had tossed my anxieties to one side, "Madame, it has been there for three hundred years" his reassurances were hollow, and at the first vibration of his digger the whole lot had fallen inward together with a lovely curved chimney in the corner which we had sighed over, since its position made putting a bathroom there difficult. When the wall fell the builder, instead of asking us before taking action, simply rebuilt it in the same place, when we would have been only too happy to have it moved to the opposite corner giving us the space we wanted... Moral: explain in tiny detail what you are thinking of doing *before* you leave for home.

There were other problems: we had asked him to install the septic tank down the steep bank away from the house itself, with its run-off buried out in the field further down where we could plant our willow, this being the traditional way of assessing the health of one's septic system: if the willow was flourishing, so was your tank!

Imagine our horror on our next visit to discover that far from obeying our instructions he had not only bulldozed away the back slope of our garden, exposing the building's naked foundations, but had also plonked the septic tank, for ease of installation, directly under the kitchen window, burying it there and terminating the run off pipe scant yards from our parking area.

Fuming with rage we had tried to remonstrate but he had already moved on, we were of no further interest save in getting his bill paid, and we had entrusted one of our friends with seeing to this, He, not understanding our requirements, had simply paid up when the job was done thinking all was as we had asked. Sometimes we learn the hard way. At others not at all...!

We decided to keep the new roof space inside completely open from end to end, we wanted to have it lined with the attractive wood finish known as 'lambris' or thin tongued and grooved planks of pine or oak which, properly done, makes a roof space attractive open, clean and satisfying to look at... or at least, it should.

We entrusted this work to an English contractor whose adverts said they specialized in such work, Mike, our local friend who we had asked to let us know when it was done, telephoned with news "You've got a ceiling" he told us. photos followed, we were pleased; two weeks later we went down... so had our ceiling, it lay in random shattered lengths all over the concrete floor, palsied ends sagged wearily from rafters, odd corners had survived giving the idea of what it ought to have looked like, the rest had simply cascaded from its place, warped and weary, and more than half split and broken.

How had this happened?

We had asked that intermediate battens be put in between each of the main rafters, with the lambris screwed onto them in order to level up the line of the finished ceiling and make a secure job, none of this had been done, they had tacked on thin battens with oval nails, and fixed the lambris with one inch 'secret' pins driven through the tongues on each plank, on the first damp day these pins, already rusting, had 'sprung' as the raw wood swelled, almost as soon as they had finished the job.

We were angry, but nothing was to be done, the contractor had gone bust and returned to England, I knew why…

I spent the following three week holiday redoing their work, perched insanely on a shaky erection of ladders, plywood sheeting, and stepladders, sorting out the tangled mess, numbering ends, battening anew and properly, and repositioning the jigsaw by putting in three thousand brass screws thanking God for the inventor of the rechargeable electric screwdriver I was using. By the end of the job I had lost pounds in weight, but the ceiling never moved again and looked splendid… moral, do it yourself if you can, don't pay any bill till you have seen the work yourself and duck dodgy Englishmen!

These blessedly were the exceptions, most craftsmen were just that: 'Masters of their craft'.

M. Comment, the joiner who undertook to make our new doors and windows was one such. He lived outside the village and rather than getting premises there he chose to use his father's old workshop out in the sticks. Often such old family businesses had used the same workshops for many years generation on generation, and saw no reason to change; at all events the drive to locate them often took us into unexpected and attractive places.

M. Comment's 'atelier' lay at the end of a series of tracks. Small fields, enfolded by hedge and copse, guarded minute areas of hay which were reaped a couple of times a year or grazed by cattle, and in the copses chestnut, oak, acacia and walnut predominated, supplying local artisans with their raw materials.

In addition lane edges were frequently piled with long undulating drifts of cut firewood logs stretching away down the road, the pieces stacked head-high. This annual harvest fed voracious fires in local homes which had been using this renewable resource for centuries.

Stoves here are often vertically inclined to accommodate the metre long logs they are fed on, they burn slowly but warmly fed via a small circular lid on which as often as not, a kettle steams, there are many of them, and each season the woodsmen cut coppice wood and stack it in these attractive piles to dry.

It was only lately that improvements had been made and free standing or 'insert' type stoves burning shorter logs had become popular, and one of our own winter joys was the job of sawing metre long logs in half and splitting them down for use, steadying the work on rough frames, it could be cold at times doing this, and we kept a selection of saws, axes, wedges etc. handy together with coats, scarves and gloves but it could be a frustrating job, as with most things, technique and practice are all!

Driving around our lanes we were always on the lookout for supplies, preferably already cut to size and split. It gave interest to the stacks of logs, sometimes half a kilometre long, lining back lanes and giving touches of form and contrast to a winter's morning drive.

It was easy to see how seasoned your logs might be, fresh-cut they showed a glowing pale ochre on the ends which began to tone down as age progressed to greyer colour, and finally on very old logs scrofulous bark and bright lichens melded with mossy upper parts giving a pleasing continuity of shade and antiquity to many such stacks.

M. Comment had refinements to this pleasant habit, his own stocks of timber were stacked in great layered piles outside his workshop, each board resting on battens to allow the passage of air during the long seasoning process which could occupy up to five years.

It was rare to find unseasoned or kiln-dried timber out in the countryside though it was gradually creeping in, especially for use in fencing and post-making, along with the growing and reprehensible use of wood treatments, engendered by the new laws forbidding the sale of properties that had not been treated against termites and woodworm.

M Comment however was thankfully, for the moment, immune to these niggles.

Inside his workshop you were in another world. Beamed roof spaces harboured dusty cobwebs, sawdust lay on window ledges and floors in deep colourful layers, and his ancient but well-loved machinery was scented by resin, oil, sawdust and the hot scent of whirring steel and singed timber when they were in use.

His work was stacked around the walls, doors and windows; solid tables, chairs, wardrobes, kitchen fitments and fruit trays a riot of form and texture giving one a chance to observe his craftsmanship as you waited.

We had been among his first customers when he started out on his own and he never forgot the work we had given him providing a showcase for his work locally, His prices had been correct, his work faultless, and we had no complaint of anything he did for us; in addition using a local artisan was well received in the village, along with the plumber, the roofer and even the builder… though we'd reservations in light of our experiences with him but generally the villagers liked us using local labour.

Our plumber was another gem, willingly putting himself and his skills at our disposal, He was an 'artisan' in every sense of the word, When it came to installing our guttering on very uneven stone walls he fabricated and bent zinc brackets to suit each position, made junctions and downpipe connections, soldered all the joints into an homogenous whole, was tolerant of our demands for interior piping and choice of toilet unit and basin, found us a double Belfast sink for the kitchen, tailored the taps to suit the barn's age and look, and smilingly repaired our main water pipe after we had severed it with a mattock trying to refill its trench. All this was watched by the villagers, no doubt discussed in the cafés, and cautious approval given.

Most seemed to know about the ceiling and septic tank, there were muted noises of sympathy, yes these things could happen to anyone – and it was only our inexperience – we would undoubtedly learn. And they were willing to be tolerant meanwhile.

I must regress a little; at this time very few English had settled in our region of the Lot, most preferred the more opulent lifestyle of the Dordogne, consequently we had been an object of considerable interest and apprehension in the community we were joining.

The farmer from whom we had bought the barn had been stunned to find two English women looking over his old barn. His eyes had gleamed with half concealed avarice as he adopted a nonchalant pose for the estate agent, but we could see he was overcome with barely suppressed excitement!

Properties at this time were on the market only half-heartedly. Nobody really believed in it, but farmers, hearing that foreigners had been looking for ruins to convert had put their buildings on the market, most not really expecting a result but one never knew, and it would be too bad if one had missed any opportunity...

Most of the barns and outhouses were unused for much of the year, especially those which had been in use for drying tobacco, once grown here in profusion until the government took away the subsidy to growers; now it was hardly worth the effort and so many of the barns and covered spaces had fallen into decrepitude.

Properties in consequence tended to hang around until the owners had almost forgotten; one farmer might sell a barn and in the ensuing months others might try a bit harder, or someone else would fall to thinking of the money they might make but on the whole stagnation ruled.

Now suddenly, for our farmer, the miracle was happening; he might have only used the barn to keep cattle over-winter and it had sat deserted for months, but suddenly out of nowhere these figures had come, ladies at that! The possibilities made him breathless! His small and voluble wife had accompanied us as we looked round, chattering ceaselessly, grabbing our elbows to emphasize points to which we were totally oblivious at the time. Later we learned that the farm belonged to his mother and the wife was busy telling us all this.

From then on whenever we appeared we were treated to the farmer's attentions, he eager to ogle his new friends while his wife regaled us with family history and showed off her grubby children, accompanied by the tiny and voyeuristic 'uncle' who spoke no known tongue but made up for it with earnest eyes and pleading gestures.

Later, when our French improved we discovered that he was offering to keep the property tidy while we were absent.

Staying over once or twice in tent or caravan, we would be aware of him prowling around at night wandering his old lands, poaching, and hoping to glimpse something.. Though we never really knew what...

Our first such night in the tent we had pitched on a level glade alongside our wood was memorable in itself for other reasons. We had excavated our fireplace, dug our cool room, selected forked stakes for lantern and kettle, erected our borrowed frame tent, and happily sat by our campfire as the stars came out, a great silence hung over the land; we were 'Home'. Just after three in the morning Jan began to be ill...we had not eaten anything suspect but she began to experience abdominal pain and be sick; ere long she was in agony, every fifteen minutes she had to dash for the wood and it was not long before she had explored most of it.

Next morning we visited the local doctor who prescribed large amounts of medication little of which was much help but we did discover the benefits of the suppository especially where the patient cannot keep anything down...

The graphic demonstration of their use by the pharmacist bought wide grins to the faces of interested waiting customers but he was quite correct, it really is the only satisfactory way of getting to the 'seat of one's problem'!.. English take note!

By the following day we were headed back north, a salutary lesson in real time about buying a property so far south. Jan was sick all the way back and we must have visited every hedge and tree and most of the roadside loos ere we reached Le Havre.

Investigation in the UK showed up a collapsed gall bladder aggravated by her tablets and a little white wine she had drunk to celebrate our ownership; as we had learned elsewhere – don't try to camp at your new address!

Chapter 4

French and Frustration

We gradually learned, including the fact that if we invited people to look at projects we could pick up quite a lot of very useful French to make life easier next time. In this we were unusual; many people never bothered to try to speak or understand the language though in some cases it wasn't always necessary, I wrote at the time:

"Mention ironmongery around Gourdon and only one person comes to mind, Patrick, master of the mundane, conqueror of the conceivable, the animated lexicon of his business, willing cheerful and knowledgeable, and above all he speaks English!

Among the vast reservoir of ex-pats resident in the area many never learn to speak French or even try to, yet they yearn to restore, renovate, upgrade and refurbish anything from tumbledown ruin to fermette or isolated cottage, and to these Patrick is as a god.

You can talk to him in your own tongue and whatever he may think of you and your ideas he is unfailingly polite. Even in the face of the grossest absurdity or with the most frustrating client, he's endlessly inventive, outspoken at times when they come up with some of their nonsense and yet they hang on his every utterance.

He knows his business from A to Z and back again. He knows what they want, what they will be capable of using, and where they can get it, he knows every tradesman within a hundred kilometres and every source of supply both locally and nationally.

He no longer works for former employers; he's gone out on his own and bought a small shop in a nearby village. It has a barn for storage, and he has put in wide windows and bought a small lorry; he will succeed because he has two great advantages, he knows his job backwards but, above all else, he speaks English..."

Our adopted village had its characters: you saw them every time you went to baker or café. There's the old lady, gnarled and bent as some witch tending her many flowerpots outside her front door, there's the old man in wasp-striped jersey occupying every day his bench in front of the Mairie, beneath the attenuated shade of a tortured plane tree, there's M. Gamby carrying another lot of designer chic shoes into his emporium, the local architect sipping his morning coffee in the bistro and of course you become known yourself.

We were the two mad English women who had bought Freysett's old barn and were making it habitable; by that time enough foreigners across in the Dordogne had done the same thing for news of it to have reached even here. Heads were nodded, after all, why not? Yes one might wish to live in a barn, we provided local artisans with work we paid our bills exactly and on time, with due regard to the ages old tradition of some of it as 'cash in hand' and this as much as anything made us acceptable.

The story of the roof lining had made the rounds, sympathy was expressed, and guarded wishes for the future, after all we would be living among them soon.

Slowly with the infinite patience of all villagers they came to accept that we might be 'bizarre' but we were amiable, reliable, and making efforts to learn the language.

Our French learned in evening classes was of little use; among themselves the locals spoke a patois and French only when they had to, for the most part we nodded at each other and enunciated what we hoped were the right phrases before both sides retired to reflect and hopefully act in whatever way was needed.

This was especially true on the occasions when we decided on having a coffee in the local Bistro; greetings were easy, ordering now easier, but where did one go from there? Clearly they were asking questions, equally clearly we were not quite getting the gist. I shudder to think what inelegancies we might have uttered in our innocence and ignorance!

That we might have a problem had begun to impinge on us

when we first began to try to talk to our farmer's wife, clearly she was bemused that anyone might not understand her: she held our arms, looked hard into our faces, and spoke very fast with frequent admonitions to the children rollicking playfully around her.. Perhaps we were the first foreigners she had met; it seemed likely, families tended to be insular, accustomed to gabbling at each other in truncated phrase and commonplace, tacking an extra letter or two onto perfectly normal sentences, and expecting us to understand.

For some months we were convinced that one of the first things she had said to us was "My mother sweeps up leaves in the park." It seemed reasonable; later we decided she was telling us that it was her mother who owned the farm and lived rather grubbily in a long low 'fermette' cum cowshed tacked onto one half of it, piles of farm junk littering its frontage, among which numbers of hens and ducks passed precarious lives till wanted for the pot,

Clearly life was basic, hard, and narrow. We discovered that the elderly mother had almost never been to the next town, and when we came to purchase the barn and we all had to go to the Notaire there to sign the Acte de Vente, it had been a singular event in her life necessitating new dress and new shoes, while the little uncle, who seemed to live with her, hovered around until the deed was done, coming with us to the bar afterwards to celebrate with gap-toothed incomprehensible bonhomie.

Yet so little did we see her normally that she might well have 'swept leaves in the park' for all we knew.

Slowly visit by visit we began to find ourselves understanding better. On these occasions we always had to go to lunch with the family and be shown off to whatever relatives happened to have called round.

These were serious occasions, we were expected to attend, offence might have been taken if we had neglected to do so. The meals were always the same: soup with great chunks of bread torn from the big round loaf, French beans cooked with garlic and oil, crunchy and tasty, big pieces of roast duck or chicken and a triumphantly produced 'Tarte tartin' or upside down apple tart caramelized and delicious and served with a thin custard called 'crème Anglais'.

Their wine was evidently made on the farm since both farmer and wife would point to their rows of vines extolling their quality one year, pursing lips the next, the red wine was sharp, not much to our taste and always a glass of Walnut liqueur followed the meal, together with the headache-giving black coffee both of us found hard to drink.

But everything was always so generously pressed upon us that it was hard to refuse, clearly they were proud of us, the cachet of two foreign ladies living on one's land was something prized, and we played our part to the best of our limited understanding smiling and nodding, shaking hands and offering cheeks to be kissed as custom dictated.

At the bottom of our lane dwelt an elderly couple in a small terraced house near the main street. The husband at first wanted nothing to do with us, but his little elderly wife was curious and probing, offering us good day as we passed, and it was she who nagged him into reluctant acceptance of these strangers.

Mind you, we almost lost the battle at the start, our large caravan scraped the corner of his beloved Deux Cheveux which he had parked rather badly in the lane but his immediate fury was disarmed by his wife, her hand on his elbow chiding him for having inconvenienced us by his thoughtlessness. "It served him right" she said, "people must be permitted to pass" and anyway we were neighbours now and he must apologise at once. Oddly enough he did, and we had no further problems, he was effectively 'tamed'.

After that several people began regular walks up the track ostensibly walking their dogs but also to see what we were up to and feed the gossip exchange, the lane was a public one and we did not mind.

They watched us shifting the dung, renewing the roof, saw the carpenter installing new doors and windows and the plumber putting up guttering, they applauded the terrace we built to one side and observed with interest as we struggled to lay a hundred yards of driveway, using a base of large stones carefully fitted together and covered in the creamy sandstone gravel from Sarlat which weathers so beautifully, and they nodded at us in friendly fashion as all these things came to pass.

We had purchased a small green tractor of the type used to mow grass, together with a bright red trailer to help us with this work. The stone and gravel had been deposited as near to the barn as the lorry could get, but had to be shifted downhill to the new driveway line. The tractor and trailer made the job easier, and served as well to bring supplies up from the farm down the lane when the track way was too wet to get the pickup nearer.

This access road was a source of some problems to us since it was in urgent need of repair, but we had discovered that we must needs be cautious about this; technically the responsibility for its upkeep was the village's, the Mairie from time to time sent round gangs who repaired the local infrastructures; all should have been well.

Our track also served a farm and another holiday home owned by a French couple who worked away from the region and came down at weekends, and according to Patrick the owner, the council should repair our track and put it into useable order, but we soon discovered difficulties.

Rightly the Mayor decided that until we were actually living in our barn there was no need for that expense, the farm tractors could use it without any problem, he saw no need for either unnecessary expense or physical improvement.

Yet something had to be done, it was frankly dangerous, sloping badly, slippery of surface and most of it overhanging a ten foot drop to the forest floor.

At the same time, whilst the Mayor was happy for us to make repairs at our own expense, he told us frankly that if we did 'adopt' its upkeep beyond basic necessity it would mean that the commune no longer held it as 'their' responsibility.

We compromised: down the road was a quarry which provided stone of the right size, we hired a small loader with a bucket to level the track, bringing several loads of stone in on our pickup to effect immediate repairs.

All went fairly well, we offloaded, raked, and spread stone, cut away the incline on the inner edge, and were finally able to drive up to the Barn on a semi-stable surface in dry weather.

What we had not realised was that coming the other way after rain, we would have to negotiate a steep and slippery descent which, despite the new stone, was still in effect a slide.

Traversing it one wet morning our pick-up suddenly began to slide inexorably towards the edge and the drop awaiting it.

I used not to believe in angels… That morning changed my mind. I had time to say to Jan "We're gone…" as the pickup slewed to the edge and tilted over. At that moment something picked the vehicle up and put it back on the track…. When we had recovered a little we got out to look. There on the muddy verge were the tyre tracks skidding outward until the outer vanished over the rim, the other a scant foot on the surface, that single set had stayed on the road, the rest of the pickup had been over the edge… I don't expect anyone to believe this, I can only say it happened, by every law of probability we ought to have rolled down that bank and been severely injured if not killed outright. Nowadays I do believe in angels…

Our good friends Mike and Jill put in the terrace, carving away the hillside to extend the area, walling it securely, and laying down the flagged surface together with its drainage system. At last we were able to dine outdoors, sun ourselves, and contemplate what it would be like when we could live here permanently.

Mike and Jill were our first English friends in the area. We met them first when they were running a 'house husband' business caring for properties in the area, doing turnarounds after 'lets', undertaking pool care and cleaning, together with small and large building projects. They agreed at once to add us to their list of clients. Mike was a superb craftsman for whom only the best work was good enough. His wife Jill had that tenacity of spirit and work ethic which makes a perfect partnership, and we grew to love them dearly both as guardians and as the good friends they became.

Mike also built our mezzanine floor for us, laying

planking, putting in stairs and balustrades, the result was very pleasing; we felt now as if we were indeed 'getting on'.

We made one mistake, ours not Mikes: we had volunteered to dig the long trench down the hillside from the nearest pipeline and direct to the barn; what we had not realised was that it was further than we thought and that we should hit red clay half a metre down.

The work was hard, but we persevered and completed the deep trench needed, helping the plumber lay the pipe into the barn via a hole in the bathroom wall.

It was a couple of days before we could backfill the trench, and next day it rained hard...

We discovered suddenly that we had created our own gushing river, for the clay at the bottom of our trench acted as a hard watercourse and was perfect for guiding the accumulated hillside water directly downhill and into the barn!

Quickly the floor flooded, desperately we strove to break the flow, divert it, and send it down another route, luckily, being on a slope this was possible, and we ended up with a pond in wet weather below the car park and a clay-stained concrete floor inside the barn. Moral: 'Think before doing'... another lesson learned the hard way...

By this time we were spending longer periods in the barn; we had put a mezzanine bedroom floor, stairs leading up to it, and railings across the end to keep it safe; we had a kitchen and 'Godin' stove, a lavish Italian creation of black aluminium and flowered panels borrowed from our Dordogne friends, the floor was tastefully clad in large terracotta tiles, much of our furniture was bought and installed, rugs garnished the floor in the lounge area, we held our first dinner party for Mike and Jill, followed by one for our farmer's family, we could drive up to the house, park, turn around, sunbathe on the terrace, we planted wisteria to climb along one wall of the barn a grapevine on the other we felt at home, we could manage guests... It all seemed too good to be true, and of course it was... In 1987 the UK house market crashed; luckily we had seen it coming and downsized accordingly, but one of our sacrifices was the French Barn...

Our hearts ached as we said our goodbyes to it and to the people who had become our friends. Mike and Jill continued to be our good friends, but we had to say farewell to the farmer and his family, our village and its inhabitants, and, sadly, our dream.

Another corner lay in wait; it only remained to see what lay around it...

Another of our sacrifices during this time was our boat. Our lives had changed and with them the need to go on living in the Haven. Sailing had been a part of our lives but it was becoming more and more expensive, a new kind of sailor was emerging: slick, attired in the brightest of clothes, brash, sure of themselves, they filled the bars and yacht clubs, their designer footwear giving them the label of the Yellow Wellie brigade among more traditional sailors; they raced at weekends, crewing the new breed of lightweight racing yachts, or owned fibreglass cruisers, two point five children and all... They were as alien to us as we must have seemed to them. It was time to sell the boat and move ashore.

Yet boats had been a focus in our lives that would be hard to replace, it was good to remember some of those times...

Chapter 5

Sea and Salad

Yacht delivery is one hell of a way to make a living; it's great if you get the long-distance warm water jobs, not much fun when you don't.

This was typical, a cold winter had seen long periods of frost interspersed with short 'clears' and long blows which kept us chaffing in port.

A delivery from Chichester to Whitby took a fortnight and we became rather too familiar with Lowestoft's outer harbour as gale followed gale; the nearby lifeboat house seemed an apt companion.

Several times trawlers put optimistically to sea only to return in an hour shuddering. If it was bad enough for them it certainly was not good enough for us!

So we stayed put until one morning a vessel went to sea and didn't come back; By that time half the port was astir and we joined the queue, sailing out into a towering swell which was on the starboard quarter and gave us a splendid shove in the right direction. There was no wind, and Whitby was a relief, even though we had to wait off till the tide made, and by then we couldn't afford any more time.

Another job awaited: this time an engineless racing yacht which had been bought by a French gentleman, and could someone, "S'il vous plait"- bring his new baby home.

She had a very full suit of sails and gear, unlike many that we had to deliver, and had solid accommodation but not a vestige of navigational gear aboard. This happened a lot: somebody sells his boat and strips her of useful gear to put into the next one, the new owner hasn't bought anything yet, the sensible crew take their own!

The first evening found us riding to a kedge off Ryde Pier in a flat calm. Avoiding a sluicing ebb tide, we rowed ashore and bought fish and chips- this could be a long one! We got to know St Catherine's rather too well as we swept gaily past; paddling didn't help and waggling the tiller just added to the circles we were making, The night was bitterly cold, we sat watches in our sleeping bags at the helm, ships swept past majestically and warmly, we weren't amused!

Two days later we raised the loom of Cap de la Hève but it took a further day to reach it, In typical sod's law fashion it began to blow half a gale and we sped into the marina under all sail to the discomfiture of several boats who evidently wondered how we would stop, Fortunately there was a spare space at the very end of a pontoon and heeling steeply we creamed into it, dropping dead on the doorstep in a flurry of terylene, we wouldn't after all, have broken an egg.

Another job awaited, this time a twenty-foot fibreglass sloop with almost no gear, to be taken from Chichester to Wilhelmstadt in Holland. By now the weather was settling into long cold spells, interspersed with fogs and gales on and off.

We had almost no spare gear at all, just a mainsail and genoa, a loo which literally 'looked down' into the sea, and a small paraffin stove to cook on.

Jan had joined me again for this one, and we motored out of the harbour in a flat calm which lasted until we reached Dungeness where a fitful breeze grew from the west and gave us a helping hand together with a fair tide as far as Dover, where we got more fuel for the outboard.

Sailing again we met a real 'pea-souper' as such fogs are called, and felt our way into the North Sea very gingerly, almost getting wiped out by a ferry from Ostend, making no signals, and relying on his radar too much; they seldom expect small yachts, and almost never slow down in fog.

By now a rising gale was beginning to build nasty seas which we surfed down with the sheets free, yawing wildly at the end of each surge. Clearly it was going to be one of 'those' trips!

Dropping the main helped for a time, but we were soon sailing much too fast, and a broach kept threatening. I was heading for the Scheldt, but as the coast neared the seas grew and grew, and it became unsafe to drive downwind onto a lee shore, so we hauled our wind and lay up towards the Oosterscheldt, reaching it a couple of hours later and finding a break in the surf, slid into the estuary.

Arriving in Wilhelmstadt we found the boat owner hopping with dismay at the fuel bill and demanding to know why we were so late.

Following this was a thirty-foot sloop from Falmouth to Lisbon; it sounded good, except for the usual lack of gear, and again no working engine. We sailed down to the Helford River on a rising wind, and with a forecast likely to put one off sailing for life!

Four days later we were listening to reports of damage to shipping, including the Queen Mary which had suffered badly, having had pianos breaking loose and several passengers hurt in falls, it was a relief to hear a better prognosis and slip out to sea the following day.

Outside, the swells were still large and the wind an angry upper-end force six bolstered by all the cold air, but it made for a fast passage and we surged into the rade de Brest on the wings of another deep depression.

The Malcolm Miller was sheltering in one of the bays and we joined her to ride out the storm; her people were kindly giving us hot showers and a supper, while we listened to the wind, and when finally we did sail next day the sea was boiling over the reefs running out to the Parquette buoy, and we kept well clear before heading south.

It was a bumpy ride though fast, we made La Coruña on the third night; I had not wanted to go in, but one of the crew had come down with suspected appendicitis and we could not take the chance. Jan became the source of some humour, I tried to find a doctor at seven am – not easy when you don't speak the language – and when she was finally carted off to hospital she says that she became the subject of a heated lottery about who would do the operation and for how much. In the end she discharged herself, and, hand on stomach, gingerly flew back to the UK, where a nice man did it for nothing!

But we had to continue the voyage and sailed on a balmy

evening bound down the coast. Shortly we were enveloped in as thick a fog as I've seen in many a year, and crept onward sounding our own horn and listening urgently for those of anyone else, not everyone uses them. All at once a darkening of the gloom revealed a grey coaster's bows rearing above us as he passed in total silence – trusting to Luck and God we presumed – he was registered locally and evidently did not expect to find anything in his track, and we ducked just in time, fuming inwardly at his neglect; later we spent an hallucinatory night convinced that we were sailing down a wide staircase, I merely report things as they were, drawing no conclusions… neither of us had been drinking, yet we shared the same illusion. I may say that under similar conditions I have found myself sailing up those stairs, as well as totally disbelieving the compass, perhaps it would make an interesting study for someone in one of our universities – they seem to have done almost everything else!

The only solution was to slide into Vigo until things improved, and we entered with care, feeling our way until we were able to anchor just off the town. On a previous visit I had been very entertained by large fishing boats curtseying in and out among the moored yachts and boats dip-netting for small fish which seemed to be shoaling at that time. One was also able to see the fog rolling down the harbour hillsides like a living thing, curling and enfilading among the trees and buildings. We looked for a clearing late in the evening but it didn't happen and we sailed out next morning to take our chances, all antennae quivering…

This time we were lucky: as soon as we made an offing the fog thinned and a rollicking breeze got up, soon we were sailing along under spinnaker and boomed-out mainsail and having one of those fabulous runs that makes all the frustration seem worthwhile as we tramped happily across a vibrantly deep-blue sea and spoiled only by the discovery that the spinnaker halyard had jammed in the masthead sheave and we couldn't free it or get the sail down. The wind was getting up by now, and we decided to carry on as long as we could. Fortunately the halyard broke, and we spent an exciting few minutes retrieving the sail from under the boat. The rest of that trip was anti-climactic in that we enjoyed good sailing down to the Tagus and berthed in the 'Belem' basin in fairly good shape, to be greeted by an ecstatic owner and his friends. After the meal he arranged for us in one of the seafood restaurants fronting the Monument, I can fully recommend the experience.

Sometimes these jobs extended into short contracts, or led us to other things and we would find ourselves spending a few months caring for someone's yacht or crewing through the season. Occasionally the work took us to places we might never have visited otherwise, one such period became our 'Venezuelan Interlude' I wrote about it at the time:

'The catamaran's awning was doing its best to emulate a hang-glider, gusts above gale force were wrenching and lifting the entire flimsy structure and it was only a matter of time before it disintegrated. This shouldn't have been happening: the boat's owner had assured us that "We never get hurricanes in Venezuela" everything was conspiring to prove him wrong.

Overhead the yacht's rigging was performing a complex series of rising shrieks and in the worst blasts the boat was heeling wildly even here in a sheltered berth under the lee of a small peninsular below the owner's luxurious home.

Sand abraded our faces as we struggled to secure the catamaran and its cover and wind-flung sand-grains were abrading the varnish from hatches and rails which only a few hours ago had been so pristine.

The rotor of the masthead wind speed indicator shot off at high speed like a banshee Catherine wheel to land in the water far to leeward, and I fell to reflecting on our immediate future somewhat bleakly.

We'd been at anchor up in the islands when the warnings began to come in, the storm had veered from its predicted track and was heading our way, it was hoped it would turn north soon, otherwise... The owner remained unconvinced, "We never have hurricanes..." he kept repeating though with less conviction as the beast kept on coming, ignoring precedent and his certainty; in the end even he had to give in.

The ethers were filled with the collective feelings of some dozens of small craft scattered out among the islands who were it appeared, scuttling for any shelter they could find and being very vocal about it, I suggested that we too move, but the owner was indecisive and it was four-thirty before we upped anchor and began our retreat.

By now a force eight was blowing rising rapidly and our berth was twenty miles to leeward, we sailed out under engine and storm jib, visibility was almost zero and torrential rain began to fall; in true sod's law fashion the compass chose this moment to go on strike freezing on its pivot, it was a hairy sail...

Seas in the lee of islands were still small, but in the gaps the full force of the storm was now flinging its outriders through them and over the beaches, we were surfing badly at speed even with our small rig.

Now, with warps out to jetty and trees on shore, fenders out all round and ropes parcelled and protected the yacht was busy sawing at them, seemingly intent on breaking her restraints."

Watching two large tankers steaming to their anchors out in the lee of the big island to windward, awaiting a berth at the refinery, I pondered once more on the circumstances that had brought us here...

'Corners' appear at the least expected of times and in the oddest of places: this was no exception.

We'd been in Palma, Majorca caring for a big sailing yacht, refitting, bringing it from a state of neglect to one where it became a pleasure to look at, as the number of quayside strollers who stopped for a few moments testified.

Among them one day was a short, dark-tanned elderly gentleman, iron grey of hair, enthusiastic of manner, who accosted us as we worked, saying that he had a yacht by the same designer in his home country of Venezuela, that it was hard to get good crew over there and, should we ever decide to move we should write to him, he felt sure he could offer us a job.

Needless to say we were not inclined, at the time, to even consider it, but later when we decided to change jobs his name sprang to mind.

We knew nothing of Venezuela except that they had a lot of oil, and occasional revolutions, there seemed no harm in writing.

The answer came when we had almost forgotten about it; a telegram awaited us in the port office and he wasted no time on unnecessary verbiage!

"Come, four hundred pounds per month, collect tickets London Airport, reply soonest."

It took a while to decide, but at that time the wages were good, and 'all found' so we sent a telegram accepting provided we had guaranteed return tickets 'just in case', and tried to find out a bit about the country itself. That being agreed we looked at each other and said "Take a chance" agreeing to go for a three month on either side trial period.

Now, in the early morning humidity of Caracas airport we were wondering what we might have let ourselves in for as we perspired and struggled through the business of retrieving our bags and finding our first contact here.

Luckily he was carrying a large placard with our name and quickly got us into a mercifully air-conditioned car and whisked us off to a breakfast of waffles and maple syrup while we got our breath back.

We were to fly on to Puerto la Cruz, though 'fly' seemed to be beyond the capacities of the battered aircraft awaiting us on the runway on our return; The throng around us was noisy and as we boarded we noticed that the two engines looked like Whittle rejects: oil-smeared, lame probably loose; once aboard things looked no better; our fellow passengers were passing the time comparing bits of seat that had fallen off and safety belts that didn't work, clearly many had never flown before...

Astonishingly not only did we get off the ground but as we looked down on the coastline below we actually began to enjoy the experience.

Lurching along at a height whose only consolation was that if anything should go wrong we would not have too far to

jump, we watched green shores, deserted bays and coves, palm
-edged beaches, a few ramshackle dwellings, unwinding
beneath us, with scarce a boat to enjoy them.

Puerto la Cruz was small, dusty, cooler than Caracas; once
again we were met, this time by a very battered jeep and
decrepit driver named Carlos.

He was to be our chauffeur and guide, but for the moment
was taking us to an hotel for a few days as the yacht was being
fumigated. A faint alarm bell began sounding in my head at
this news as we checked in…

We spent a week cosseted to the point of boredom,
exploring the town by day and swatting mosquitos by night,
and came to know the town well.

Supermarkets had armed guards patrolling and it was no
uncommon thing we were told, for them to open fire on
shoplifters. Small urchins swarmed, who regarded their day
wasted unless they could part us from some of our wealth or
simply grab at our clothing to get attention. They were many
and we found the contrasts between rich and poor very
pronounced.

Finally however we were taken to the boat. She lay out in
the old Salinas we were told, and the journey began among the
shrub and flower bordered residences of the well-to-do
degenerating the further out of town you went, tarmac
vanishing, houses thinning, growing more and more scrofulous
until we were travelling through a wasteland of hardened mud
ruts along a narrow road between clapboard shacks, cardboard
shanties and filthy drains till it petered out completely and all
at once we found ourselves poised on the rim of a landscape
unfamiliar to any save astronauts training for the moon.

In front of us over an area some five miles by three, the
earth was being torn apart and carefully recreated; giant
earthmovers trundled around dwarfed by the scale of what they
were attempting, gouging long channels and bays from what
had been a salt marsh, depositing loads of rock and earth into
mounds between the channels, and systematically reshaping a
small hill into rising terraces and scarps, the whole scene
dominated by a confection of tiered rock which Carlos told us

was to be the centrepiece of this development.

But to reach the yacht in those early days whose white masts rose incongruously from this desolation, we had to follow a muddy and winding track which it seemed was in the habit of changing at short notice. Carlos rode his bucking steed rather as Don Quixote accepting neither delay nor hazard and we veered crazily from rut to rut dodging rampant bulldozers and grinding trucks with ourselves rattling about in the back like balls in a raffle draw as he gunned his aged engine, waving to everyone impartially.

In this manner we arrived. A small wooden jetty protruded into a creek inhabited by large numbers of pelicans and egrets, and stunned, we surveyed our new home.

To seaward lay islands in the distance, nearer at hand was a small beach, a minute shed, and lots and lots of Nothing, no houses, no trees, no buildings, no slipways and no boats save for a small alloy catamaran on the beach; blue waters, green islands, and ourselves; it was as if, used to the overcrowding and bustle of the Solent, you had awakened one morning to find everything had vanished and you had it to yourself.

A yachtsman's dream, but there was nobody to enjoy it.

We had been told that there were two Carib-Indian crewmen who lived locally and these shyly introduced themselves, affable to a degree, they swiftly offered us cool drinks and withdrew forward.

There were language barriers of course, but these began to go down under mutual effort and a small nautical dictionary I found, so that soon we became masters of "Drop the anchor…" and "Stow the awnings!" Despite the recent fumigation – or perhaps because of it – our chief enemies in the days to come were the cockroaches, reared in a special assault school, these had, it appeared, virtually taken over the ship. To enter the galley at night and put on the light was to reveal a frozen tableau of poised legs and quivering whiskers and to sense that it was we who were intruding and they who owned the joint and were its rightful occupants.

We squashed and sprayed, fumed and fought but we never won. Isolated pockets of resistance quickly became massed battalions: our defence was prolonged, and useless. Against this backdrop we came to know something of the boat and her crew.

The boat was splendid, a lovely American ketch sixty feet in length with plenty of power under both engine and sail, she was a real lady and quickly won our affections. The crew were a different matter.

Both hated rain, the smallest shower saw them heading down into the focsle unwilling to work outside, but to us the greatest sadness was the owner who had suffered a stroke because of which he had lost enthusiasm for the sea and seldom wanted to sail the boat, preferring to go everywhere under engine.

It was very unfortunate and not his fault at all, but we were seldom able to use the boat to her full potential.

The Islands however made up for these minor problems as did the sailing when we were able to do some, winds were generally light to moderate and tended to be predictable we went out two or three days each week and as the owner loved his waters we would explore along the coast to windward or down to the Islas Espiritu finding deserted sandy cays where we were frequently the only boat, unless a charter yacht happened to have come down from Grenada for a few days.

Navigation too was mostly un-complex; usually the pointed thumb and 'about there' bought one to the destination in due course. Our favourite island group was the 'Islas Caracas' and there we spent long days and nights in solitary splendour until supplies ran short.

Even so with such a wealth of marine life one need only drop a line over to have snapper crowding on board, The crew liked to take the yacht's dinghy and dive for conch out in the channels, preferring the shellfish to meat. Squid could be had by the dozen if one hung a light over the side. After dark, Langouste too were plentiful, yet the owners often chose to eat expensive made meals rather than what was available, while the crew and ourselves ate what was caught and tended towards the basic.

Jan however was often driven frantic by the unpredictable

behaviour of guests who, having ordered a midday lunch might appear at three pm expecting hot food to be ready when salads would have been far more appropriate to the weather or have her efforts greeted with "Oh we're just going swimming...." which often meant a wasted meal, still we managed, but we often felt they did not heed the consequences of their lack of thought as we sometimes had to throw food away because of the heat and lack of a large enough refrigerator to keep everything fresh.

However there was plenty of work to do on the boat: the under-deck head linings were coming apart in the heat and had to be laboriously remade panel by panel, but chief among our problems to begin with were the boat's toilets.

These were standard marine units but when we arrived we were told they had been troublesome, we stripped and checked them sweating in the confined spaces, and discovered that the two-inch copper waste pipes were almost solid with lime-scale reducing them to a scant inch of clear pipe, no wonder they were troublesome... judicious hammering with a wooden mallet gradually broke up this accretion, but it was a wonder they had worked at all!

On one occasion a guest lost a linen handkerchief down the loo and, embarrassed, failed to tell us; it took five hours of intricate frustration to discover the problem and hack it free from the rubber ball valve it had got tangled around; linen deserves its reputation for toughness. I still shudder at that one.... Marigold gloves did not seem adequate for such a job, and unfortunately the loo had not been flushed properly at all!

There were many compensations; some of the mangrove encrusted creeks with their tiny village communities were incredibly lovely. We swam from palm-fringed beaches on which the only footprints were our own, we dived among coral gardens of fantastic variety, we rambled uninhabited islands and cays, we swam in the evenings, despite the owner's cautions about marauding barracuda, sometimes we followed hammerhead sharks through glinting blue seas, turtles occasionally swam around us – in short, our small voyages were idyllic.

On the few occasions we managed to persuade the owner to sail we would put up the spinnaker and surge deliciously through gentle seas rolling rhythmically, and anchoring at night after such a day's sail could be very special.

We had, on one occasion, sailed up the coast to a place where we could haul the yacht out and clean her bottom., A thick layer of marine growth had accumulated, and once she had been freed of it and repainted she raced like a swan. On the way back we were lucky enough to pull into one of our favourite anchorages for the night in an almost circular bay out on one of the offshore islands.

Bonito and flying fish accompanied us as we motored in having enjoyed the glorious sail, and relaxed and content we spent several days anchored here.

As dusk fell one evening two outboard-propelled fishing boats came in and the crew, a family, set up camp in the lean-to palm-thatched hut at the head of the bay. Later the men came out to us asking us to trade salt and coffee with them in exchange for goat meat; the exchange over to our mutual satisfaction they returned to the beach.

It was a silent star-filled night, their fire burned low on the beach and finally went dark. We slept out on deck – humidity was high and we preferred to leave the cabin to the owners and crew – for once I was glad we had chosen not to go below.

I was woken early in the dawn by sounds from the beach. An elderly woman had begun to add sticks to the fire and prod its embers into new life in a curl of blue smoke; a dog played with a small black pig along the beach and the ancient grandmother came down to the water's edge and washed her face before wading out to one of the boats and returning ashore with a large fish.

She was filleting this when two small children emerged rubbing their eyes, their voices sleepy and slow; unaware of being observed, they were natural and uninhibited. Soon another young woman joined them, followed by the men and soon they were gathered around the fire eating and talking in low voices.

By now the sky was a blaze of gold and blue above the low

seaward sand-spit and the smoke of the fire swirled against the ridge till caught by the land breeze and whisked away.

Their meal over, the family began to make ready for the day, the men went out to the boats and began mending nets, the younger women picked up machetes and moved slowly up the slopes of the hills around the bay on their way to cut firewood which presently they began to throw down to the grandmother and children waiting below to collect it up and carry it to the lean-to.

Scenes like this must have gone on here across many centuries, it seemed an appealing if hard way of life but clearly they knew little else and were content. Perhaps it's only romanticism but somehow it seemed very desirable compared to our own restless and fraught ways of starting our day.

Sadly our time here was coming to an end, the owner deciding to part with the yacht. Times were changing, and we would need new employment, but that early dawn seemed to encompass all of our experiences in this place: its silence, its struggle for subsistence, the palm-fringed shores and intimacy of countless families going about their daily affairs in such simple ways, It epitomised the peace of the islands. We might be going, but we took powerful memories with us; watching sand blowing across the bay as the tail of the hurricane swept past our mooring place I knew we would not forget our Venezuelan interlude…'

Chapter 6

Fleabites

Palma, Majorca did its best for us on our return for we arrived to find an irritating problem facing us – the boat was overrun with fleas....

It had happened because a local ne'er-do-well had chosen our boat as a comfy doss house whilst we were away and when he was finally shooed away by the local jetty guard had left this awful legacy behind. When we opened the hatch on our return the problem had been all too visible, the interior seethed with dancing life! We called in the shock troops with their sprays and powders... They got rid of one problem but left us with another: we couldn't possibly live aboard in the stench their treatments had produced and we decided then and there to move ashore for a time and overhaul the boat completely.

We should have had to do so anyway; months of idleness had seen a thick marine growth cover the bottom and when we tried to motor over to the slipway the boat moved painfully slowly.

The shipyard owner goggled as his men hauled the boat out on the slip, she sat solidly upright as we had assured him she would, without chocks or blocks of any kind, perched on her great wide keel; a few blocks satisfied safety and his pride, but were not necessary.

The growths were thicker than we had realised, and took a lot of chopping off garnering great piles of shell, tubeworms, barnacles, sea squirts a small octopus and assorted marine life ere we were done; we scrubbed her clean and left her to dry as we began on the inside.

We had rented a flat to store our gear and somewhere to sleep while all this went on, deciding it would be a good chance to bring Jan's mother over for a holiday in the sun. We met her at the airport and she took to Majorcan life at once, coming into town with us each day and discovering little back street bars where she held court to admiring audiences, all fascinated by this upper echelon refugee from Milton Keynes who spoke not one word of Spanish but she seemed to make herself understood and was evidently popular with their clienteles...

Over the next two weeks we staggered home each night reeling from antifouling poisoning, and stained, lumpy, and blotchy, but Mum was in her element! At the end of her holiday we sent her happily home clutching her souvenirs while we re-launched the boat and readied her for another trip-all we needed was a corner to look round...

Necessity saw us spending one winter moored in the outer harbour of Tarragona. This ancient town had many attractions, but with funds low, we left them to the influx of tourists and tried to keep our heads down both financially and practically.

We should have been moored snugly alongside the town quay, but a newly-arrived and officious Port Captain disliked yachts on principle unless they belonged to the very wealthy and banished us to a berth inside the fuel terminal pontoons where we had to put up with a slick of permanent oil, tankers arriving and departing, and still pay dues as we would have on the more salubrious mooring.

By this time most of the half-dozen or so yachts had decommissioned for the winter, some owners taking advantage of the six-month rule to return to England or Holland, not to return until spring.

Indeed it was beginning to become difficult, The law said you might spend six months in any country after which you had to move on to another, or lay-up your boat and its gear for the following six months, Many people were having trouble, since officially even house-owners had to obey the rule, and either let or close up their properties for a period relying meanwhile on friends or fellow travellers to tend their properties or craft while they were gone.

This left just three of us in residence, caring for the others' boats, and refitting our own during the winter months since our legal time span differed from theirs, and we in our turn would have to do the same thing later.

Normally this would have been ok, but this year severe storms swept the coast and we were hard put to keep everyone secure as swells swept into our corner laying a nasty black layer of spray-flung oil over our assortment of craft.

However we persevered, pestered at odd times by Spanish Customs looking for drugs, and by one very unpleasant episode which occurred one day quite early in the morning.

Without warning heavy feet clattered over the pontoons and decks, and the hatch was flung open to reveal a pair of sub-machine gun snouts unwaveringly fixed on us. We were ordered on deck and held there while the excited Paramilitary Police searched each boat thoroughly, paying little regard to possessions, everything was flung casually around and left there, the normal Guardia just stood by watching and we got the feeling that nobody interfered with these boys!

Slowly they began to calm down, deigning at length to explain. It seemed that a prominent politician named Carrera Blanca had been assassinated in Madrid and it was believed that foreigners were behind it, hence 'all' foreigners were suspect, and treated with little consideration until proved innocent, the search was for guns, explosives, papers – any incriminating evidence.

Having seen how uptight the paramilitary Police were, we thought ourselves lucky not to be involved, and to have in our possession the right documents covering our present stay in Spain. Jan had insisted on this as an insurance against just this kind of harassment but several locals including holiday home owners who had not had this foresight were sent packing, or even had their homes confiscated.

This officiousness was something we found hard to cope with, for it ranged from a complete lack of interest normally, to intense and uncomfortable encounters such as this whenever a new broom or local police chief thought there might be mileage in chivvying foreigners and their properties. This was quite common at the time in Spain and the attitude of the local Guardia could be very unpredictable as we had already discovered, either they joined in the fun or completely ignored it till it suited them to intervene.

We had had another similar experience along the coast in the port of Motril. When the single Guardia came aboard he demanded to see our papers and our passports, He sat, big, brash and intimidating in our small cabin thumbing through our documents but saying nothing, scrutinising them again and again and laying them on the table before him, sitting there just staring at us.

Nervously we offered him a cooling drink, he accepted but carried on fingering the pile of papers and looking us over, we wondered what we could have done to invite such scrutiny! Nerves tingled unpleasantly.

Finally as if making up his mind he smiled and gently pointed at our newly arrived mail lying on the table, what could he want with that? What he wanted was the stamps from the envelopes. Shyly he asked whether we had any more as he was a great collector... Our relief was profound and yes. He got all the stamps we had on board... luckily we had saved them for a friend, but under the circumstances! Whew!

Such episodes tend to leave one feeling nervous about officialdom; rules were arbitrary, changing often, and it was hard to find out exactly what pertained in any given season. It paid best to have all one's documents in proper up-to-date order, and as far as possible we always did this, it helped to avoid unpleasant episodes.

The following season we decided to go back to France for the winter months, this time to Toulon where work awaited us, helping refit an aged but lovely old sailing boat for a Canadian owner. She needed everything from complete repainting to new decks, gear, and interior furniture, and we spent a happy few months giving her a makeover such as she had not had in many years.

By the end of that job it was nearly Christmas and we decided to spend the holiday in a fashionable resort we knew of just down the coast.

I wrote "Christmas St Tropez: in wintertime the town

becomes almost tranquil but today weather chops short any other options; we'd anchored off the small bay of Canobiers beneath the old town but strong winds from the direction of St Maxine made the berth untenable and we moved into the shelter of the harbour.

A French yacht coming out smoked past as we went in, her crew supine along the rail; freezing, saturated and grinning broadly, they waved happily as they smashed into the short steep seas coming across the gulf under reefed sails and with torrents of spray half hiding the boat and her reckless French 'Sportifs'."

At the quayside we were welcomed by and teamed-up with the crew of a Canadian yacht newly-arrived who, as the day progressed also invited us to join them next day for Christmas lunch.

We were touched therefore, after a superb meal, to be presented with a mascot for our boat. They had seen the yacht's name, and the carved ivory walrus tusk they gave us stares reproachfully down as I write. It had been around the world with them and everywhere else with us, but seems to find this current sedentary life rather trying.

Of course we've moved on a bit – thirty five years and a lot of sea and land in between – we have moved from yachts to motor homes, to French houses and now to this little home here in New Zealand.

We shared a lot with that family, joy in companionship over the holiday, both of us in a strange place; they were outward bound again on another world trip in their new craft, built by themselves, we were told, on an island near Vancouver and launched on ropes vertically down a cliff. When we went over to Canada last year we tried to find the place and them, but without success, and our time-frame was too narrow to allow of further explorations. Next time maybe... meanwhile our memories are strong, St Tropez, the family and that Christmas lie a good way astern... but still very much in our hearts.

Chapter 7

Italian Interlude

One of our jobs involved taking a rather aged motor yacht from the Lebanon to Italy and remaining with her for the summer season in Naples, Despite her many problems we finally left Beirut and had a tranquil trip as far as Rhodes, bypassing Cyprus, which at the time was in the throes of yet another of its periodic upheavals as Turks and Greeks disputed territory.

At the time Kyrenia where we had intended calling in, was under military rule and visitors were not very welcome. Rhodes offered a much better haven.

It might no longer have its fabled Colossus, supposedly transported away by a Jewish merchant in pieces, but it's not hard to imagine it astride the harbour entrance, nor to recall the island's subsequent turbulent history from its classical period through Romans, Byzantines, and the Templars who fortified the island and made it their home for two centuries until they too were ousted by Suleiman and the Ottoman besiegers. Unusually for that time the defenders were allowed to depart unscathed by their chivalrous conquerors and take with them such wealth as they could carry. In 1523 therefore, the knights departed and left Rhodes to the Ottoman Turks who converted many churches into mosques and on the decline of their own empire, let its buildings fall into disrepair.

The yacht we were on had been here before. On the last occasion she had managed to wipe off a couple of stabilizer fins and this had left her decidedly cranky. Diving in the clear waters we established that she had lost two of her fins on the port side, so it was rather bad luck when a stray Meltemi decided to hit us halfway across to Naxos after we sailed, and the following few hours proved rather instructive and not a little scary.

I wrote at the time:

"A shrieking wind grew out of the Northwest, it didn't begin, it already 'was'. It just came. The yacht shuddered under the initial onslaught, heeling savagely, loose 'somethings' clattered below deck, the sea smoked."

We waited, our thoughts engaged upon each of our particular domains while the question hanging in the air was "Is this a local blow or part of something bigger?"

I checked mental charts; had we emerged from the lee of anything? To windward lay a lot of islands but none which might have been sheltering us and none very close.

Swells already long and high were growing alarmingly, a shorter vicious sea building on their backs making the yacht stagger drunkenly. The useless stabilizers mocked us; I'd known she would roll – ninety feet long and a mere fifteen wide, she was like a log – and with the weight of two heavy speedboats and big outboards on her upper deck she was sadly overburdened.

We nursed her, keeping her head to seas and praying that the engines would keep going and that she would not slew beam on to them: if she did she would quickly capsize.

We kept her hovering all night, steering by feel rather than sight. By now visibility was less than a hundred metres and all we could do was jog into the seas, gentling her through them as best we could. Dawn bought no relief except it gave us an horrendous view of what lay around us. The pumps were beginning to fail and every time we plunged into the seas the props raced and had to be throttled back lest they tear themselves and the shafts apart.

All of us matured a little before we got into the lee of Naxos, where we were able to take stock and select the best potential refuge into one of the tiny bays on the island of Ios into which we crept most gratefully.

The blue-capped sugar-icing church welcomed us into peace and tranquillity. The silent beaches and rocky shores were a balm we needed badly after our dusting outside. Sadly Ios has since been overwhelmed by package holidays and tourists, but at that time the three old men depicted on tourists postcards still sat on the bench observing it all, hands clasping their sticks.

We stayed long enough to recover, but the boat was beginning to leak badly and her pumps by now were working intermittently; it was time to move swiftly on.

Athens when we reached it, had already suffered the fate of Ios, and smelt to boot. We had to go there in order to refuel as this had not been possible in Lebanon, and before I knew it we were embroiled in an argument with the port authorities in a row about supplies and over an anchor which had been inadvertently dropped near the port's underwater telephone cable. Heavy hints of retribution were calmed by stoic promises of future good behaviour and a promise to disembowel the engineer responsible – if we ever caught him!

Full of fuel and seen off by a suspicious launch we made shift to one of the places I had always wanted to see: the Corinth Canal.

At an early age I had been given a book in which was a colour picture of a steamer viewed from above, wedged into a narrow waterway with scant inches clearance, and I had vowed that one day I would travel it.

The real thing outdid my expectations. We paid our dues to the hovering official launch and waited our turn – for the traffic is one-way – sure enough suddenly from out of the rocks a ship began to appear like some stupendous conjuring trick; she just seemed to slide out of the background as if grown from the cliff and shortly after we were marshalled into first place for our own passage, giving us a wonderful unobstructed view.

Ahead lay a ruler-straight cut with steep sides disappearing in the distance and we nosed cautiously into this dramatic drain.

Sand blown from the sides whipped along the decks, while below the waterline we could see rocks streaked with paint left by close caresses from passing vessels, some of which were rather large, many a shipmaster must have had hysterics as his vessel rubbed along with nasty noise accompaniment from below.

Halfway through, a bridge spanned the cut high up above, and little cut-out people waved to us as we passed beneath their feet.

It was a relief to emerge safely from the other end, and we headed towards Corinth happy that we had saved the alternative long trip round the peninsular.

Corinth itself proved to be silent, dusty and deserted. In silence we moored to an old jetty and in silence walked into town to find a telephone. It was of course lunchtime, and nothing moved.

But a crisis loomed: the yacht was now leaking badly and the pumps had given up the struggle. The engineer suggested that as he couldn't get suction on the manifold, and the hand pumps were inadequate, the crew should turn to and bucket it out, but the film of oil this left on the waters told us it was time for sterner measures, We compromised, getting a road tanker to pump out the bilge water, and then heading as quickly as possible for Corfu where we were told we might find new parts for the pumps, We nearly didn't make it but not due to the leaks. Off watch and asleep I woke with that pit-of-the-stomach sensation that momentous events are unfolding, and raced up to the wheelhouse. Just as well I did, the lights were very close and the boat was headed towards a white line of surf!

Hard astern, hard astarboard and full ahead got us out by a whisker, and we resumed our journey with steam emerging from the wheelhouse. So much for hired crew fiddling with the heading marker of the radar rather than keeping a lookout...

But the weather was good and the leak had scared itself so that we were able to enjoy a tranquil journey, islands appearing from Homer's 'wine-dark sea' the heat haze over them soft and downy before they again vanished in haze astern.

Ithaca giving me a few heartaches as we passed, I recalled a book by Ernle Bradford in which he had sailed his boat Mother Goose on these same waters. I longed to do the same, and to land on the island but at least I was close by. Ulysses seemed very near and very probable that each headland might conceal bank-oared triremes, Jason's ship, the Argonaut or some sheltering deep-laden Phoenician trader.

The engineer spoiled it by coming up to say that the flywheels were spraying water everywhere but Corfu was close and we would soon be in port, where another tanker could relieve us of our irritatingly oily bilge water.

A wonderful and generous-spirited Corfu inhabitant found a repair facility in the back streets and a local electrician rewound the duff motor. The leak was partially traced to a faulty inlet valve, its oily component to a loose sump plug, and the pumps were soon back in action, though we had to get in another tanker to relieve us of the noisome mix of water and oil. The only difficulty as we finally departed for Italy was caused by our main anchor dragging home in a sharply rising wind as we were recovering it, causing a few anxious moments to our immaculately painted neighbour ere we got clear, My sincere apologies to 'Black Swan' and her crew.... but at last we were outward bound once more.

The passage between the mainland of Italy and Sicily through the straits of Messina was disappointing: no sign of the great whirlpool just a few scattered swordfish boats, and a flat calm sea with occasional swirls to indicate that it might be a very different place in rough weather.

Coming to Naples from the south one finds the Isle of Capri on the one hand and Sorrento on the other; we made the passage on a sun-glazed morning with the Calabrian mainland blurred by mist and the sea sighing wearily, its surface flecked with iridescence- not as a natural phenomenon, but due to patches of oil (not our fault!) but very light and mobile. It was our first encounter with the pollution which seems never to go away.

The Bay doesn't cleanse itself easily, therefore if 'romance' is your idea then close your nose to the miasma and opt for more airy climes.

Mind you, our own ship was still little better: persistent engine problems had smeared her on the voyage from Corfu, with a thick sooty deposit from her two exhausts, and a great clean-up was needed ere we could go into haven.

Our berth was to be in the new marina at Mergellina, along

with several other large yachts, and we found ourselves very much marginalized to begin with and berthed at the end of the mole. The port was chock-full of expensive craft, most of them idle playthings, for one seldom saw them go out.

Owners tended to come down to their boats at weekends and spend long afternoons sunbathing or drinking on their broad afterdecks, lounging contentedly on their designer cane furniture, cooling drinks within reach, any idea of actually putting to sea never entering their heads.

Later that evening we discovered that we had also become part of a comedy. Our berth as has been said, was at the end of the mole which protected the port, while at its head lay a transient village of fishermen's huts, hauled boats and drying nets, and of course promenaders, who took their ease every evening with a promenade along the mole in large numbers and commented as they strolled along, on the richness of the craft lining the jetty. Now we too were objects of interest, a new exhibit and of interest to the many Neopolitans taking their evening stroll, meeting friends, making assignations and generally behaving as only Italians can.

'New days, new ways' we decided. We were about to become a part of some 'New ways' long before the 'New day' dawned!

As dusk fell a long grey shape slid quietly out of the harbour, the Customs were prowling it seemed and everyone watched them go as twilight descended.

A last ferry came in from Ischia, its weary passengers dispersing into the city from the terminal and peace ensued, but not for long…

At eleven-thirty we 'sensed' rather than heard a couple of dark shapes slipping around the end of the breakwater from seaward and making straight for our new berth; there was a muttered "Scusi Senoras" and suddenly our decks were alive with swift figures forming a long line and beginning to toss cartons quickly from hand to hand and so to shore where other waiting figures stowed them into vans while the promenading walkers egged them on eagerly.

All this happened in unusual silence, the Italian is not noted for being quiet but these people were; in no time the first boat was slipping away again, another taking its place, They were long and sleek, their exhausts burbled, almost silently, in twenty minutes they were gone.

We were informed that on the morrow all these smuggled cigarettes would be sold cheaply on the streets. It was routine: the Customs launch disappeared, the smugglers watching their opportunity hastened ashore, the deed was done and everybody was happy including the local police who ransacked the fishing village at dawn in retrospective and semi-serious fashion. The game had been played, honour upheld on all sides and in the morning we found a carton of free smokes left discreetly behind a ventilator, along with a most delicious bow of thanks from the leader as he departed.

We could never complain that Italian life was going to be dull....!

We quickly learned that other details here were as flexible, The ear-ringed 'pirate' who tended the quayside water hoses ran a tight racket. One's water bill kept going up until you protested, when it would come back to normal before beginning another spiral. He always seemed perfectly happy with the arrangement having neither sympathy nor shame, profiting wherever he could until faced-out, then the game just began again till the next time you argued.

Another version of this opportunistic nature occurred when we visited Capri. Looking for a mooring spot in its busy harbour we were guided in by a cap-wearing and satchel-bearing individual who helped us tie up, gave us a list of fees and collected the dues smiling cheerfully as he left..... No wonder!

Ten minutes later we were embroiled with the real harbour authority berating us for being in a ferry berth. We should have to go and anchor outside... we came to learn that these lovable rogues always smiled as they robbed you. It was all very slick and good humoured!

At which point I must introduce you to Joe... He came to us on a temporary basis while we were in the port, appearing on the gangway one morning as we refuelled, a grubby American sailor's hat crushed in one gnarled fist and he was asking for a job.

Joe it appeared had done everything, sailor on merchant ships, deckhand on yachts, he professed to be able to 'Hand, reef, and steer' as the old salts had it.

As it was, not much of this was true, but we needed a hand and took him on anyway while we were in Italy.

Joe proved to be a walking disaster. Not only did he have no idea about anything marine, but he was dominated by his wife, of whom he was terrified; encountering the lady later in a small dispute over pay scales we came to understand his anxiety. She was vast, dominating and tenacious; she left us feeling grateful we had survived the interview and eager to please her thereafter.

If Joe could get anything wrong in his work he invariably did so; let us be hauling on a line to free a fouled anchor, Joe would be standing on it, as bar-taut the rope creaked in anguish, his first attempt at washing the chain as it came aboard saw him tumble head first into the sea, and later, he was seen standing out on the very end of a quivering gangplank, rope in hand and holding his hat on while trying to toss a mooring line ashore. Needless to say he failed.

Sent to clean down the speedboat lying alongside he studiously cleaned everything from the stern to the bow, finally cleaning himself right off the end and into the harbour where his little hat floated all alone; fearful we went to his rescue, but he'd got himself to the gangway and crawled out a drowned bedraggled rat wondering what had happened.

Coming up from Capri in the speedboat we would bring our gas bottles to refill. The boat did about forty knots flat-out under its huge outboard and Joe sat in the stern clutching his hat in one hand and embracing a couple of gas bottles, a look of terror on his poor face, He later told us it was the most exciting thing he'd ever experienced, and boasted of it all along the quay as if he had done it all himself, especially telling everyone about the fact that we had beaten the big hydrofoil on the trip up the bay.

Joe was also a voyeur; we discovered this when two of our female guests decided it was too hot to sleep in their cabins and chose instead to have mattresses moved to the upper deck where they went happily to bed. Next morning we heard a shriek and investigating found Joe happily ogling the ladies while industriously hosing down the deck all round them. Later, finding him missing, we discovered him varnishing a ladder over and over again with his head poking up above the deck level as he enjoyed the girls sunbathing topless nearby.

In the end he had to go, but it was amazing how much we missed him for a time, and it can be infuriating having nobody to blame for things when they go wrong...

Ischia provided us with one of our periodic stopping places, entering its volcano-crater harbour was to be transported back in time; it would have been no surprise to encounter a trireme emerging through the narrow channel leading into the port, and surely some of those houses had been here forever. Timelessness bathed us at every hand. Our debut into the port moorings had been tinged with drama; I had asked about a space and was told that it got very crowded inside the harbour especially in season.

On arrival we discovered the quayside a solid phalanx of visiting craft. There seemed to be no room anywhere and after a moody circle or two I decided to heed the advice I had received from the harbour master and try anyway.

Dropping the anchor ahead I put our ship into reverse and shut my eyes. Astonishingly there was no bang just a gentle scraping as the ranked masses somehow parted like the Red Sea to Moses. Crews frantically moved lines and fenders to avoid our steel stern looming like a battering ram at their seemingly immovable line. In ten minutes we were moored. We had arrived!

Of course there's always a bit of a kerfuffle of outraged dignity among the other inhabitants after such manoeuvres but we were within our rights and sulking deckhands soon scrubbed away the evidence of our mild caresses, some verbally as well as physically; but it quickly died and we became part of the scene, expected to co-operate when the next visitor appeared.

A storm was brewing, the engineer had finally gone too far in many areas and to save the impending explosion if he remained with us, we contrived to get him transferred onto a luxury yacht which was just leaving, convincing him what a step up it would be and generally nudging him and his baggage towards the gangway as fast as possible lest he miss the lift.

Peace descended, we grew to know and love the little town and harbour, its lovely ancient buildings, its market, its small shops, and transient boating population. It felt very much like Home.

Punctually every morning the ferries begin arriving, bringing with them their loads of tourists who fan out through the island taking over the town and its shops, attractions and cafes.

On some of days we would exit the port and sail round the coast to the Spiaggia de Cartaromana or its 'beach' a volcanic area of hot springs off the coast. Here we would spend the day diving in clear and deep water finding a fascinating undersea world around us.

Another of our favourites was Procida, halfway to Naples, where in a bay on its southern shore we found limpid shallows and were able to clean the yacht's bottom from all the marine growth common to these warm waters, and which grew at an alarming rate. Snorkelling and using an air buoy with two breathing tubes and masks we were able to do this job in a day, easing the problem of having to haul out in some shipyard at huge expense; Italy we were discovering, was never cheap!

A little incident epitomised our stay here; we had gone up the coast to anchor overnight out at the entrance of a small bay. As darkness fell our attention was attracted to something happening in the village at the head of the bay where colourful fishing boats were hauled up on slipways and a low quay provided wharf space in this tideless sea.

All at once the church bell began to ring softly and as it did we began to see many figures kneeling at the water's edge.

Shortly we could share in what they were doing, as borne on the land breeze, a myriad coloured lights began to move across the calm water towards us in long wavering lines, the candles flickering in coloured paper lanterns set on pieces of Styrofoam, each a small 'boat' which drifted slowly down to us till we were surrounded by dozens of bobbing multihued lights.

Prayers were being intoned by fishermen, villagers and their families as they set their offerings adrift, and for some while the procession of lights twinkled its way towards us, the leading floats by now snaking away out into the Bay of Naples in undulating curves as wind and current took them. At last they were gone and we went silently and contentedly to bed, glad to have been a part of the celebration, touched by its simplicity and the deep devotion of its participants.

Chapter 8

Africa

When I was seven years old I was removed from the chills and depression of a gloomy post-war England, and found myself together with my family, boarding a Union Castle liner from a vibrant and freezing dockside shed bound out for 'Darkest Africa'.

I knew it was 'darkest' because Billy Smart had been at pains to tell me so "You're goin' to 'darkest' Hafrica my Dad says…'e reckons you'll 'ave to 'ave a torch ter see wiv…."

Thus my young expectations were coloured by his claim. It seemed reasonable – we had heard of darkest Africa in geography class – it had never occurred to me that it might be other than gloomy in consequence.

At that age one tends to take things literally…

London's docks were alive with vessels. Liners, cargo ships, tramps, tugs, lighters and barges… an urgent frantic scene, snow sifting down through the early glare of gas and electric arc lamps, skeletal cranes dipping and swinging, grinding along quayside tracks or hovering above open holds, emerging with beaks full of bales and boxes or slings full of sacks, while the mournful siren of a new arrival seared the evening gloom.

The voices of the human cargo were muted amid the cacophony, among them a gaggle of well-wishers huddled into overcoats and scarves; even now a few paper streamers linked ship to quayside, and underfoot a deep throbbing in the bowels of the vessel and Blue Peter flying stiffly among the whirling snowflakes against a brownish gloom laden sky spoke of departure immanent.

Cold it was but no colder than the lurching journey in Granddad's upright car with its bonnet-mounted temperature gauge, no colder than chilled fingers grasping favourite toys, no colder than the pinched faces hurrying along slush-rimed pavements or poised momentarily above steaming gratings.

And surely no colder than the many hearts parting from loved ones for who knew how long? But leaving little to be said and no audible voice with which to say it.

Breath steamed, gangways were being lowered back to the quayside, the last crane sighs and nods into stillness. Only the swinging wires and pendant hook tell of the recent activity.

Lines splash into translucent green water cast off by those who will be staying behind, a tug sobs and jets dark smoke as her screw threshes into brief and turbulent movement, our bows ease out slowly while a few last figures watch and wave as the gap between ship and quay widens, kisses are thrown from gloved hands to unidentifiable faces; a few gulls accompany us to the lock where other figures who would soon be home before warming firesides ease us out into the river where, alone in the enfolding darkness we softly nose down lonely reaches lit fitfully by flashing buoys and occasional pools of spangled luminescence betokening industry or habitation and which rapidly fade into deeper darkness.

Bronchitis, a congenital winter problem, saw me hustled off to my bunk where I remained on and off for several days, save for one morning when, swathed in overcoats, I was allowed to see the serried ranks of the Alps in the dawn light glowing pink and gold in the early sunshine.

The sight induced in my young being a sense of wonder, of beauty, a sense of 'belonging' and a yearning to know more, for in that moment was born my ongoing journey as a Mystic lover of Nature in all her manifold guises.

Genoa was almost as cold as London, pistol-carrying police huddled miserably into greatcoats; very few of the passengers even bothered to go ashore it was simply too icy, but as we left port once more a watery sun began to appear and by the time we passed Stromboli glowing in the darkness it was palpably much warmer at last.

Sicily passed, and next morning we were off Alexandria, white and pure in early sunlight.

By the time we reached the Suez Canal I had discovered real sunshine and bliss of bliss, 'warmth' at last!

I couldn't remember ever having been really warm before. My early memories were composed of freezing draughts from the bowels of an open ground floor hall and stairwell, which whirled around our own first floor flat, with its bare bedroom floors, a token smear of linoleum in the bathroom, and meagre sitting room fire in front of which washing on a tall drying rack took precedence over people. Frost decorated the window panes in winter into ethereal fern patterns inside as well as out, low wattage bulbs provided a gloomy light, and a single bar electric fire might briefly be put on to take the chill off a bedroom before retiring, all else seemed equally dispiriting. The streets were lined with hedges, high, dense and dripping with moisture through which a watery sunlight seldom percolated.

These memories vied with long chill waits at tram and trolley bus stops on the way to and from school, stamping icy feet and blowing on numbed gloved hands to keep warm, then the slow agony of thawing, the pain repeated again and yet again each frost-blighted early morning.

Now, suddenly, I felt as if I had been translated to paradise!

The passage through the Suez Canal was pure magic. Not only was I warm but there was the added vision of seagoing ships traversing a desert endlessly fascinating, while small urchins waved and yelled enthusiastically from the banks and their elders either ignored us or raised laconic hands as they carried on with their work.

As part of a convoy we maintained a set speed and distance apart but the organization was evident, the convenience of the canal made clear. The equivalent voyage would have meant the long journey around Africa by way of the Cape of Good Hope and taken far longer and indeed on our return on leave, this was the way we went.

But for now Port Said and Aden fascinated us children with their myriad bumboats, their shouting crews importuning, cajoling or sometimes bullying unwilling passengers into concluding a sale, endless strings drew merchandise up and down, money was exchanged often by tossing to outstretched hands, haggling was concluded noisily while young boys yelled and dived for flung coins into the murky harbour waters.

On board a couple of 'Gully-gully' men – itinerant magicians – charmed with their tricks no doubt cheating a little but with great good humour, eggs were discovered in children's ears, coins palmed, it was all smiles and one could only be amused by their endless efforts to part sceptical passengers from their cash.

The journey down the Red Sea was notable chiefly for sunburn. The crew had just erected the ship's swimming pool, and everyone was taking advantage not always wisely. Fresh from England, our pale skins burned easily and I was not taking much care in my newly discovered joy in warmth. I quickly succumbed, learning the hard way that sun could be damaging and Calamine lotion very soothing; it was a good lesson in bronzing slowly and I was eagerly drinking it all in as a thirsty camel might drink deep of water at a desert oasis... for the time being I had found my Heaven.

I came to love shipboard life. To me our vessel was a living thing, alive and with a deeply sensed throbbing heart of her own, evident in her vibrations, through the hiss of air in her ventilators, in her bright lights, and in the pulsating depths of her engine rooms, only rarely was she ever still.

The routine in those days was very simple. We were steerage class passengers who were getting an assisted passage and warranted few luxuries. Our meals taken in the big dining saloon were plentiful and for us children memorable because, starved by the war years of anything like tropical fruit we could hardly believe such plenty; even an orange had been rare and if we saw one it would have been in the toe of our Christmas stocking. Here we might actually choose between an orange, a banana, or piece of pineapple, there were slices of mango and paw paw, even grapes and dates, all new to us and all delicious.

Mid-morning saw one of my favourite moments when we would get a big mug of hot Bovril; this again was a joy after so many years' deprivation and to add to our pleasure as we reached warmer climes, ice cream was served every afternoon from big round tins by the stewards from their pantry serving hatch, and we kids all lined up outside grinning happily and hoping for 'seconds' which occasionally we got…

Such minor events might seem very ordinary now but in those post war years, deprived as we had been of nutrition or treats, they were new, vital and exciting!

We also loved the 'crossing of the line ceremony' This took place whichever way round one went, crossing the equator was seen as a momentous event deserving celebration. Members of the crew dressed themselves up in robes and 'Neptune', usually played by one of the officers, had a crown made out of a big margarine can turned inside out and tastefully cut into points. His 'wife' was our deck steward draped in skirt and jumper top with the obligatory 'lumps' and we youngsters were proudly admitted to Neptune's realms duly smeared with dabs of paint and grease and with a gentle push into the pool by one of his entourage.

We all got certificates to say that we had been admitted to his domains and would now be respected by sharks and whales and all other fishy denizens, being true children of the seas.

The less fortunate among the ships' crews also had their ceremonies, a lot less gentle than our own, and minor wounds and abrasions, together with nasty cocktails of pastry and engine oil, paint etc., were their unfortunate lot, but they were roundly cheered by passengers and crew alike and grinned painfully as they went off to clean themselves up.

After a life of knowing nothing but chills and fogs, colds and bronchitis, the sea and sunshine were wonderful to me, and I never got over that first love affair with ships. It has continued to this day and nothing pleases me more than boarding a vessel at the start of another sea voyage, with all its excitements and pleasures ahead.

The journey continued and as it grew warmer yet we were able to marvel at colourful clad inhabitants in the Sudan, and held speechless by a night of unbelievable beauty anchored just offshore at Zanzibar as the horizons were seared by sheets and lances of flickering lightning which exploded from every quarter and illumined sky and sea in a dazzlingly prolonged display with the scents of spices rich in our nostrils and borne out to us by a light breeze coming off the land.

Dar es Salaam, our final port of call, welcomed us to an Africa few of us could have imagined – Billy Smart had been wrong – Africa was filled with colour, and 'light'

We had come to grow peanuts; Dad along with many more had contracted to be part of the then 'Groundnut Scheme' an ill-fated attempt to provide a prolific and reliable source of vegetable oil for a war weary and deprived British population, As we debarked from the ship we found that our train was waiting and we became absorbed for the next couple of hours into the noisy polyglot mass of humanity which now enfolded us.

Chiefly native it ebbed and flowed around us as the will took it, jabbering and shrieking in a myriad tongues and dialects conducting their manifold affairs publicly and vociferously in a bewildering volume of colour and sound.

Some passengers like ourselves were boarding the train, others heading off to town or on trips; gharry drivers and vendors chaffered and bargained, imploring, cajoling, cursing and importuning; others selling fruit, sticks of sugar cane, bread rounds and unhealthy looking brightly coloured fizzy drinks in grubby bottles, yet others bearing cans and battered tins to the front of the train, returning with hot water from the engine to make tea or clutching stems of bananas; there were mangoes in wicker baskets, fruits, nuts, the dried meat called biltong, while yet others tried to persuade us to buy carvings, beadwork and gourds, leatherwork and woven baskets called kikapu, many laden with small eggs, mealie meal, and a dozen other necessities; while yet others toted bright fabrics, or colourful cottons and silks, everything calculated to attract, sustain, nourish or pander to the wants of the many passengers and visitors now crowding onto the train.

The chances of such a scene of organized chaos in, say, East Croydon seemed utterly and impossibly remote.

Tall blanket-clad tribesmen carried dangling live chickens

and stayed aloof from swift tongued itinerant vendors. Among the masses one saw Arab faces, light and dark skins, baggage-laden porters, women with water pots or bags and bundles, people trying frantically to locate their possessions while yet more families boarded the splendid and quivering train.

A shrieking whistle from the engine – a mighty smoke jetting Beyer Garrett – and a confused clash and jerking of couplings indicated the moment of departure. Those who were late flung themselves onto steps or whatever purchase afforded, others ran alongside anxious to conclude bargains or get their money ere we were gone as our engine shuddered into motion and its coaches gained speed leaving many distraught traders in its wake, as we moved slowly out through the palm gardens and picked up speed.

Once we were underway a river of people began moving in endless flow and counter-flow along the corridors, chattering and bickering, eyes and teeth flashing amid a soporific backdrop of chatter, quite wearying to our tired young minds full-sated with new experiences.

I fell asleep in the middle of a laugh, my sister curled her legs under her and dozed. Only Mother sat wakeful, wondering no doubt where this strange new journey would take us and filled with her own thoughts, hopes and fears for the family's future.

We were wakened by a bell; a smiling face looked in: Tea? The train was running now through a dry and open land of plain and distant hills, clumps of bush and trees dotted about, together with occasional scattered rocky outcrops tufted with scrub.

From time to time we were aroused by the sight of tall giraffe feeding on the thorn and once by eland racing alongside the train until they veered off in a small cloud of dust. It was very hot, all but the strongest of thought withered; for the most part we were silent. Africa enfolded us in its vastness as in a cloak and left us drained by its immensity.

The groundnut scheme to which we were bound had evolved when one Frank Samuel came up with an idea to cultivate groundnuts for the production of vegetable oil.

Britain postwar was suffering from many shortages. A team was sent to report on the area and did so favourably, recruitment began in earnest.

At that time in England, with its manifold deprivations many were looking for new beginnings. Ex-servicemen were two a penny and despite rebuilding combined with new projects, work was still scarce. The scheme seemed heaven-sent, but the project was beginning to experience many difficulties. It was much harder than anyone had imagined. Country and climate, soil and equipment, and above all the weather patterns all conspired to make it fraught with difficulties and by the time we got there in April 1949 things had deteriorated. Still there was hope; it was felt that the problems could be overcome, but few had realised the pitfalls it faced.

Kongwa, our destination had been built by those who preceded us. By the time we arrived it had the semblance of a township, so that at the end of our journey we found iron-roofed buildings, workshops, a church being built and housing going up around the skirts of the hill. Dad had already been there some weeks so we settled in quite quickly and we were lucky enough to get one of the bungalows at the foot of the hill near the church for a time. Soon we had a factotum called Alban a tall native who claimed to be cook, dhobi-man, gardener etc. and who became part of the household, though in fact he did not stay long, being found unreliable, and he was quickly replaced.

It was only much later in life that I started to question this, at age seven such things seem normal, everyone had 'boys' as they were called, and they were just another part of a new and different life.

There was also a school which we attended, although moving out fairly quickly to 'Italian camp' made getting to it a bit harder; thereafter our school transport was the back of a three ton Bedford lorry with a canvas hood which picked us up every morning and delivered us home in the afternoon.

Our morning journeys were occasionally enlivened by the lorry being pursued by a belligerent rhino who seemed to regard it as a challenge to his territorial claims. It must have made quite a picture, we yelling children, our driver accelerating madly to outpace his pursuer, his hand on the horn to scare the beast and the rhino thundering along behind in a cloud of dust till he gave up amid cheers from the nervous passengers.

Schooldays were good. We were fortunate in the staff under the leadership of the headmaster Mr Thwaite and we were able to learn some Swahili under a native tutor who came in to help us with his language. At that time things were still a bit dot-and-carry, and the headmaster and his colleagues did all they could to foster stability and school spirit, I am happy to say that the values they instilled in us have remained to this day, as has the school itself, after a bumpy period later, when it was used as a training camp for guerrillas for a time.

One of our Saturday treats was to climb up to the experimental station and there have a cold drink of water. It was something that took a lot of getting used to; one did not just turn on a tap if you wanted a drink; all water had to be filtered and this was a laborious process taking all night to half-fill the still. Everyone had to use it sparingly so these occasions when we got half a glass of sparklingly cold water up at the station were very special.

Naturally we also contracted most of the local ills too. Dysentery was commonplace, malaria too, despite Mum's efforts with nets over the bed. One of my pet hates even now is the whine of a mosquito and memories of days down with the sickness. I also got tick fever later which caused some anxiety for a time.

Locally there was a store or duka where we could buy sweets and basic items; but if you wanted to shop anywhere other than at the local store you went off on the trip to Dodoma, where a wide range of Indian run shops catered to every need, For some reason one of these families was known to my parents and so every time we went over there we were invited to dine with them. I learned early on that very hot curries did not suit me, especially when they had chilli peppers in them, but with yoghourt and milk, coconut and poppadoms the experience could be made bearable to my untrained palate, and I looked forward to the friendly hospitality of our hosts.

They were strict Sikhs, observing all the rituals of their culture and the father with his beautiful beard, iron bangles and colourful turbans was always a delight to me. They were unfailingly welcoming and courteous.

At other times we would go off on safari. There were destinations near and far; one of my favourites was to an area where a hillock of rocks was reputedly home to families of leopards and monkeys; one was always enjoined to be very aware around its margins and not stray on one's own.

On one such trip I got 'bounced'. We had been hurtling across the plain, sometimes shaken by corrugations, occasionally as here, diving into a dry riverbed or 'donga' and rattling up the far slope to crest the rim, often bouncing over humps as one did so. We always enjoyed these trips, the family was together, Dad in good humour as he piloted the borrowed vehicle, usually an open Land-Rover.

It was therefore a great surprise all at once as we bounced over one of these humps, to find myself hurtled out of the back and landing hard on my behind, only to find myself sitting in the middle of the track watching the Land-Rover disappearing in a cloud of dust. Africa suddenly seemed very alien and big, and I felt very alone! I was very grateful that my sister who was in the back with me had seen my plight and had alerted the adults before I could be left too far behind.

One of these trips took us occasionally to Sagara where there was a big swimming pool. I recall a time when we set out across the plain till we reached a place where recent rains had created a big lake across the track. Dad, being wary decided that we should not risk it, but drive around the edge, and of course we immediately bogged down in 'black cotton soil' a soft and glutinous mud, and there we stayed stranded trying every means to get out but failing and becoming very dirty in the process; by late afternoon when another Land-Rover appeared we were all filthy. Of course he drove right through the lake without any problem and courteously hauled us back onto firmer ground but by then we were far too mired ourselves to have continued to the pool and sadly turned back, weary, grubby, and much wiser.

Another of the pleasures of such travel were the roadside markets where one could buy eggs in woven baskets, vegetables and fruit, questionable meat, wood carvings, leather and beadwork, small pelts, sticks, spears or brass-work, and occasionally dicker with the locals for more exotic things like leopard pelts and genuine beadwork.

Of course today the buying of animal skins is frowned upon and rightly so, but then it was just part of life in a country full of new things, and I still have a python skin from a snake Dad killed under the walkway from the kitchen; such was all part of African life.

Eventually the groundnut scheme died its long overdue death, and we had to look around for something else. Dad wanted to stay in Africa, so while we went off on leave to the UK for six months he relocated to Kenya and found work with East African Railways, so that when we returned it was to a new life, a new country, and problems which shortly saw me staying with Mum while my sister went with Dad. Though we were reunited some while later, it created a division which was hard to heal.

Chapter 9

Endgame

It was dusty behind the settee, the leather was old, the wall damp and beetles had burrowed deeply into the planking and riddled the floorboards, but it was our refuge; we children had to lie quietly there while the adults went softly from room to room holsters open fingering their side-arms nervously.

They had very good reason, living as we did in the Eldoret region close to the Aberdares we were in the middle of Mau Mau territory. Somewhere close outside in the velvet dark terrorist gangs were targeting both white settlers and their own people in an orgy of vicious killing which made sense to no-one but themselves.

You never knew when they would come; the only warning might be a sudden silence in the night sounds outside, a cacophony of different calls as the night creatures went about their business, then all at once stillness as if the bush were holding its breath, at such times you looked to your defences.

We had to keep away from the windows, but often as we lay in bed we would hear the adults having their supper and this too was a time of danger, for the Mau Mau had corrupted many servants who, bringing in the dishes from the outside kitchen, had also been known to bring the killers in with them.

Trust, even of well-loved and long term 'boys' was very tenuous, the threats they endured directed at their own families made this an evil for which we could not blame them even while trying to retain a semblance of normality amid fearful times.

Two Turkana guards lived out on the wired-in veranda at night, but the same problems applied, if one was wise one trusted nobody, that way you lived a bit longer but there were many nights when we never knew if we should see the dawn, for we could take nothing for granted.

How close we came to becoming victims I am not sure but we had our alarms and, living in a remote area where the gangs operated on a regular basis I believe we were lucky on more than one occasion whereas at least one of our near neighbours was not.

Grim reminders were common, the terrorists turned on their own people, massacres such as those at Nyeri and Kirinyaga left one feeling sick and helpless; occasional stories of courage, as of the two elderly ladies who saw off a group who came to kill them, gave heart to others who, like ourselves, lived far from township and security.

We became familiar with the back seat of our parents' car; every so often they decided to go out to an evening at the Thompson's Falls Hotel and we had to go too, we could not be left in the house alone, so we spent long evenings with just the roar of the falls in our ears, nervous and unhappy as we clung together.

It made for a strange life, constantly wary, ever vigilant, even going to the loo was a trip in itself as it lay away from the house, and, whilst ok in the daytime, could not be undertaken at night; so we got used to commode and emptying routines, and to not roaming very far away from the house, for although our servants were reckoned to be fairly reliable one could never be completely sure.

Out in the surrounding bush was not a good place to be, though the boys often protested that if they came with us all would be well, but the risks were too high, and reliance upon someone's fidelity, even after several years, stretched us continually, leaving us unsure on many occasions.

My sister managed now and then to get a ride on 'Spotty' the horse belonging to our friend, but even then care had to be taken and he never went too far.

It was clear that the servants felt the strain of all this as much as we did, often expressing their loyalty tearfully. They had been with the family for several years since well before the troubles, and regarded themselves as part of the household but our cook was Kikuyu, and we knew that like many of his people if the terrorists had threatened his family he would look to them before us and we couldn't blame him after some of the horrendous acts the gangs had committed against their own people.

Even at school things were controlled; our boarding school was fenced around, its dormitory blocks lay behind layers of wire fences, which were patrolled at night; we were prisoners and it had to be that way.

One school overlooked a beautiful salt lake which in season was pink with flamingos which it would have been a joy to visit but again we could not do so. Our freedom lay in the kites we flew far and high, and in the confines of the playground beyond which we dared not go.

Only on brief holidays down at the coast could life relax a bit, I grew very fond of Malindi and the creek ferry we had to cross on, which was operated by a cheerful bunch of grinning Africans hauling the rickety craft across by hand, improvising songs about their passengers; often the songs were about the families who were crossing and we children, making up the words as they sweated and strained at the ropes.

Local waters teemed with colourful fish of immense variety; the mangroves were home to fiddler crabs, and the beach at low tide would be a mass of these, all gesticulating with their big claw, but make a movement and they would vanish as if a scythe had swept across the sand and mud banks. We fished and swam, snorkelled and played along the beaches or lay supine beneath the coconut palms. After the restrictions of our daily lives such holidays became very special to us.

One day a big Arab dhow arrived and anchored out in the creek, and for some time there was great activity as it took part in the making of a film called 'West of Zanzibar' starring Anthony Steel. For we children the climax was the attack on the dhow by a flotilla of canoes filled with warriors waving spears, noisy and very exciting, reminding one that such scenes were all too real and commonplace not so very long ago.

Now and again other experiences from that time surface in my mind, one such was Gedi.

We visited the ruins on a sweltering afternoon when even the encroaching forest seemed to be gasping; set some seventy miles to the north of Mombasa it was a ruin, a large walled town deserted over three centuries ago and locked within its bush setting it became forgotten until 1948 when it was rediscovered. It was this recent event as much as anything which prompted our parents to take us there.

It was called 'The mysterious city'; exuberant growth had almost reclaimed it, vegetation had overcome and covered many of the buildings, and made it hard to discover what it had looked like.

Now great matted root growths together with encroaching trees had mantled the city, the mosque and some pillars and cisterns had been uncovered, but it was still like treading into a Tarzan movie – the place dominated – if you had any liking for mystery and lost things, it satisfied every urge.

We wandered among its ghost-haunted ruins: fallen masonry, torn pavements shattered by roots and vines, coming upon dark and sudden openings whose interiors might hold any treasure, or terror! Tombs were being discovered as well as artefacts from some of the houses, bowls and dishes, wells filled with debris and some of great size, half concealed by undergrowth so that rails had been placed around them to avoid accidents.

Enjoined to beware of snakes, we explored gingerly but eagerly, and the impressions left upon me have never quite faded, for I can still see and hear in my mind its eternal sights, sounds, and silences, the long ago legacy of its Arab builders who were part of the chains of settlements along the coast.

Every season dhows came to this coast from Arabia borne on yearly monsoon winds, armadas of high pooped lateen-sailed vessels across the centuries brought dates and fish, returning with cargoes of slaves, ivory, pelts, spices from Zanzibar; every creek had its shrines and forts, mosques and tombs, or cities like Gedi lost across the ages, some even now perhaps still to be rediscovered.

Looking back to those days seems almost dreamlike, life was different and always new; coming back to England some years later seemed anticlimactic, we no longer 'fitted' for the vibrancy had gone; very few had seen what we had seen, or could even dream of such experiences. It was as if we had been to another planet and, returning, had become enmeshed and stranded in timeless mediocrity.

Small wonder then that we couldn't settle. As Kipling's soldier found out, it's hard to knuckle your forelock to the Squire when you've seen the sunset over Kilimanjaro, seen thousands of zebra and antelope flowing across a plain in seemingly endless streams, watched elephant and lions in their natural habitat, or drunk from coconuts straight from the tree. Somehow Bognor or Blackpool lose their charms by comparison.

Chapter 10

Convenient Canals

Canals have always attracted me. I used to wake to the sounds of narrow boats put-putting along the Grand Union canal in my first few years, going to the window, one caught glimpses of them between the bank-side bushes coming and going to and from the Midlands, London Docks, or between factories making pottery, mills making paper, and transporting coal and coke, bricks and cement, lime, timber, and pig iron. So canals formed an ever vibrant backdrop to our early lives.

We grew up with them, fished in them with bamboo rods and bent pins, stealing Mother's best button thread for our lines, and often hitched lifts between locks on narrow boats laden with the produce of a nation, or riding high and empty as they travelled to and fro.

The lives of their crews fascinated us, The whippet-lean bargemen, a lock-key thrust into the wide leather belt, sturdy arms winding at paddles or thrusting at recalcitrant lock gates.

Then often they'd leave the pair of boat and butty to the wife, and cycle off along the towpath to get the next lock ready.

Many of the womenfolk were amazingly broad in the beam considering the confined spaces some had to live in, hefty arms hauled at ropes, or steered, bringing to mind the barge woman in The Wind in the Willows, these women involved in affairs below, or dealing with infants while steering. Many of them wore wide skirts and aprons, though trousers after the war were taking over, but earlier, lace was often to be seen trimming broad brimmed hats, though latterly it was no uncommon thing to find the wife sporting a flat cap like her spouse, and doing her share of the lock work.

Boatmen's families often lived ashore, but gradually folk moved aboard especially on independently owned barges and as a consequence many children seldom ever went to school at all.

Almost every barge had its own unique painted ware, a decorated funnel, buckets and pitchers, teapots and jugs, and water barrels; the tops of cabin doors also came in for decoration with colourful roses and castles, and tillers were striped diagonally on powered boats while butties often had quite elaborate paintwork and Turks-head rope decorations.

In wintertime bargees had particularly hard working conditions, towpaths became icy, canals often 'smoked' in the early mornings and the cold must have been very bad.

I recall one winter when the basin opposite Croxley Mill froze over and many pairs of boats became stranded for a time, cabin chimneys smoked and planks linked barge to barge, no-one could move until an icebreaker came to shatter the blockage, and one by one they were able to slowly follow in its wake.

So canals were intimately part of our young lives and it was no great stretch of imagination to consider using them later on when we needed to get from one side of the country to the other.

We had bought a new boat, there was however one small problem, she lay stranded on the bank of a creek up in Cumbria.

One longish holiday opportunity offered, during which we might get her afloat, using the spring tides over a coming bank holiday weekend. Accordingly we made our plans and went up carrying all our gear, arriving in time to dig trenches under the bilge keels on either side and insert long sheets of corrugated iron on which we might be able to 'slide' our new vessel to the tide edge.

The 'Ratty', the miniature railway running from Ravenglass provided a tractor, and with its aid and a lot of heaving by sundry local helpers we hauled our boat down towards the creek to a point where we hoped she would float off on the next high water, Thankfully she did.

We had bought her during the longest spell of hot calm weather the country had seen for some while. We debated trying to get through the Caledonian Canal or sail west-about round the Lizard and reach the Thames that way. Neither suited very well, the one being a long way north, the other a long haul in itself and there had been no winds for many days.

In the midst of this conundrum I thought again of canals but this time specifically of the Leeds-Liverpool canal which, together with the Aire and Calder Navigation would allow us to cross England via the Ribble estuary, the Rufford branch, and so out at Goole on the Humber estuary.

Careful checking established that the canal was wide enough and deep enough for our keels and that the bridges would be passable with our mast laid above the decks on the horse and tabernacle. All seemed set and with the help of a Land-Rover at low tide we erected our mast on the hard ready for the journey down the coast to the canal entrance on the Ribble.

The trip was uneventful save that we had to motor the whole way, reinforcing our choice of taking the inland route. If we didn't we would simply run out of time before the voyage could be completed and have to leave the boat somewhere for a time, which in turn meant that we'd have no home, for we had already sold our old boat and if we wanted to keep its berth for this one we would be paying mooring fees as well. Necessity makes a good third head when choices need making.

One night spent in the harbour at Fleetwood then we were off early next morning crossing Morecombe Bay, seeing Blackpool's Tower through the heat haze and arriving late in the evening at low water, A handily moored and deserted small tanker in the estuary made a good platform for lowering the mast again and we remained alongside overnight, motoring into the canal sea-lock at high water next morning.

Readers of my book 'The View from Here' will have come across canals before but this journey evolved a little differently from the sun-seared days we knew on our way south from England to the Mediterranean.

This one began with us having to haul the yacht bodily along sections of the weed-choked Rufford branch from the estuary sea-lock the eleven miles to Burscough Bridge, due to choked water inlets and a propeller which swiftly resembled a green football of weed and left us feeling like refugees from a re-make of 'The African Queen'.

All this in a raging summer heat wave which saw water levels falling, weed growing like wildfire and our chances of success fade further as two mindlessly wearisome days passed. Locals saw two large ladies clad in swimming costumes each with a rope over her shoulder hauling their 'Barge' one from each bank like Egyptian slaves! All we needed was a 'barge' a 'bale' and Paul Robeson!

The Leeds-Liverpool canal when we reached it made a welcome change though its levels were still very low, but at least there was no weed and keeping to the centre of the cut we could progress well. The searing summer heat had caused problems all over the system and by the time we reached Wigan we had discovered that they were 'half-locking' on the Wigan flight to conserve water. That is to say they only used just enough water in the double chamber locks to float us over the sill of the next basin before shutting the gate and raising us the rest of the way. The 23 lock flight took all of one blazing afternoon to ascend, but only with help from the lock keeper, and a couple of locals who took turns on the paddles and sluices.

By the time we locked out of the last chamber the pub at Top Lock was franticly busy and, tired as we were, we had no wish to mingle with the social crowd; instead we moored to the bank 'up-cut' and after a quick supper fell wearily asleep.

Two things happened, the cat absconded ashore overnight and we had a major job to persuade her to return and, in trying to start off next morning, we discovered that our boat had been asleep herself all night long on a large double mattress!

This had wedged itself beneath the keels and, because of the falling level, was now effectively preventing us from moving. It took an appeal to the next lock upstream to flush enough water down to lift us clear, when the offending article floated drunkenly to the surface before subsiding in a mass of bubbles.

There is a difference between taking a shallow draught

barge through a canal and taking a seagoing boat; our biggest problem was that we had the keel and two bilge keels protruding below the surface, ideal for getting ropes fouled-catching fridges and gas stoves, and trawling any other detritus such as plastic sheeting or bits of rope and wire: all of these things became annoyingly apparent over the next few days.

At each bridge we became accustomed to the boat suddenly 'kangarooing' as she hit dumped domestic hardware, with freeing plastic from the prop which tangled with depressing regularity; or if that were not enough the immature youth of Lancashire had invented another game 'dive-bombing' using themselves as ammunition and usually on the blind side of a bridge so that we became accustomed to small bodies and great splashes descending from out of nowhere, urgently swimming ashore before we hit them, as they indulged this odd insanity.

We couldn't stop easily but they seemed not to understand this at all nor realise that we had a whirring propeller at the stern of the boat which could deprive them of minor limbs or digits in a trice, and we had several near misses, scared faces suddenly close alongside as they realised their mistake.

However in fairness after one such incident, the lad involved decided to make up for it by cycling ahead of us for the rest of the day and preparing locks and swing bridges for our passage; we never got to know his name but decided that every boat ought to have one! The difference it made was very evident and eased our progress considerably. Bless you wherever and whoever you are, we are very grateful.

Blackburn and Bolton surprised in that, while much of them is still derelict, there are great efforts at reconstruction being made and the canal-side warehouses and factories are becoming designer chic apartments. To southern minds these areas have always been associated with mills, smoking chimneys and back-to-back housing. It was good to see so much changing; grimy canals cutting through the backyards of towns don't always give a proper perspective of possibilities or enhance the communities they serve, so the renewal was very refreshing to see and will bring life back to both canal and city when completed.

It still seems amazing to us that we could bring our sailing yacht right across the middle of England in this way. Clearly folks as we went along were equally puzzled "What's that thing then?" became a common question. Most were fascinated, especially by the long alloy mast lying along the length of the boat, its rigging tied neatly to it, booms tucked into the bundle.

In fact this mast was about to cause us some amusement; we reached the Skipton tunnel at lunchtime and carefully checked that no other boat was coming though ere we went underground.

For a short while all went well then, lacking proper lighting, we found ourselves benighted even though we could see the distant glow of the tunnel's far end. It was stygian black in the middle, and as I tried to keep on course the boat was swerving from side to side within the narrow tunnel and the ends of the mast were hitting the sides of the roof, each blow ringing out with bell-like clarity in the confined space. We emerged eventually breathless and worn, only to discover an interested group of boats and 'boatees' awaiting us, clearly they had been bemused...

'We heard you a-coming for ages! Wondered what it were, never heard 'owt like it! By heck they'll never believe it at t'club when I tells 'em about this!" But on the whole they were very kind....

Not many can have traversed Ilkley Moor by yacht 'Baht 'at' or not. The canal wound around the contours of the hills through deserted countryside giving us long lovely views, but by the time we reached Shipley and civilization again we were beginning to have problems. Our gearbox was becoming a trifle erratic to say the least.

We'd come in for a good bit of chaffing as we went, but it was all very good humoured. We grew to like the sturdy Lancastrians and Yorkshire folks with their lovely sense of fun; everyone was very kind, and we made some good friends on the way.

Just as well, we discovered some more of this kindness

when we broke down about twenty miles from Leeds. The gearbox decided to throw a wobbly and left us without any drive to the prop; typically it was a Sunday but along came a small motor launch out for an after lunch promenade on the cut, and he towed us all the way into the city.

Bless him too, he would take no thanks or reward it was just another of the kindnesses shown to us on this and many another canal journey.

However our problem was serious and Jan was soon marching into town preparatory to hopping on a train. She said later it was one of the most scary things she'd ever done. At that time the Yorkshire Ripper was on the prowl and she had to walk along deserted dark towpaths under the motorway junctions and across narrow lock-gates before she reached light and safety; however she was back late next day after an epic trip to Stuart Turner's factory in Henley-on-Thames to collect spares, and after a hectic and grimy tussle with our heads down in the bilge re-assembling the gearbox we were back in business and ready to take on the Aire and Calder Navigation.

The first things to strike us as we joined it were its size compared to the narrow waters we'd been used to, and its colour, for it was reddish at least on this section, and well used.

Tankers, sand barges, and barges of sorts seemed to make up its traffic. Locks were large and remotely operated, no tugging at gates or winding and heaving at sluices here; everything was quick, calculated and precise.

After a time one almost missed the hand operated locks; these reminded us of some of the more modern systems in France where one's first encounter with a lock was often via a hanging pole suspended on a wire above the canal: turn the pole and the whole system operated, locks emptied, lights turned green and one motored in. The main difference in Europe was the small cabin found over there where one operated the controls oneself in many places.

The locks here were much too businesslike and impersonal, and we erected the mast again at Goole with relief at being free of them. The trip from the junction at Burscough had taken us five days.

It was good to be back in tidal waters and we made a swift passage down the Humber stopping off at Grimsby to dodge some bad weather overnight. The bare bones of this once busy port saddened us but as with fishing everywhere that was the price paid for overfishing and quotas, in vessels laid up, crews out of work, ports hushed, docks deserted save for a few stragglers fighting a losing battle to stay in the business they and their families had grown up with.

We sailed next morning into a thick fog, seeing nothing until we edged inshore to discover ourselves to be off Cromer; five hours later we were still off Cromer so powerful was the tide, and only slowly could we begin to make progress as the fog lifted. Yarmouth provided a night's shelter among the oil rig supply ships, an uneasy berth with these great lumps manoeuvring in and around us in the darkness, the sound of propellers very loud. Sound carries underwater rather too well and we were constantly startled by the seeming proximity of the ships. We sailed next morning into a clean calm day, motoring down this ravaged coastline, aware of the toll nature has taken upon its villages, at least one of which lies beneath the waves, before weaving our course up as far as the Orwell where we anchored for one night off Pin Mill; sailing again with daylight we traversed the sandbanks guarding the lower Thames estuary and by good luck with our timing, were able to catch a favourable tide upriver. Tower Bridge and the enfolding and familiar lock seemed very comforting after our saga, and there was joy in seeing our new home lying alongside in her proper berth after her epic journey.

And of course there were always other 'corners'- other places, other times, some of them the very stuff of which dreaming is made...

Chapter 11

Birthplace of Dreams

I never see Gibraltar's Rock without lively feelings of excitement. It can be the haven at journey's end or the crucible in which dreams are formed, focussed and distilled or abruptly quenched. Once upon a time you had to sacrifice to the Gods before you ventured beyond its narrow strait; even today one still mentally does so as you pass safely into calmer waters or struggles to make the offing you need for any voyage to the westward.

To understand Gibraltar's place one must climb to its summit and there shading eyes for the long view consider its importance across centuries of peace and war.

On a clear day there can be no perch which fires imagination in the way Gibraltar can do. The air may be still with that breathlessness which foreshadows great events or strong winds may whip at your clothes turning the glittering strait into a madness of tossing whitecaps and sudden whirlpools, a sea that knows little of pity for sailors, indigo, silver, deceptively dappled with dolphins at one moment, or slate-dark and menacing. The Rock is the gem amid its changefulness.

History lies just around this corner, a glance brings immediately to one's awareness the panoply and richness of the passing centuries. This rock has watched a myriad comings and goings; its passing was feared by early seafarers and the straits have become history in themselves, overseeing Phoenicians, Greeks, Romans, and Moors. Explorers and conquerors come and go while traders, slavers and many more took the myriad wares of the Mediterranean lands abroad or returned, often wearily, with hard won and sometimes even stranger cargos.

Even today there are few of us who set out from here

without our hearts a-flutter, often with long voyages ahead and who knows what of danger and adventure over the next horizon? It has always been thus.

The casual visitor coming in by aircraft or cruise ship will know nothing of the underlying world lying here in the shadow of the Rock, but come in your own boat and the story is very different.

As your yacht slips in between the piers of the breakwater and sails rattle down, there opens a vista which in a few days will become as familiar to you as any home street. I wrote at the time:

"Any day in Gibraltar's harbour: Overnight a couple more yachts have come in and now lie silent and at rest in the old destroyer 'pens' which serve as space for visiting boats, and among a motley gathering of craft of every description. Sleek motor yachts, trim modern sloops, a couple of old gaffers, converted fishing boats, ketches, yawls, a schooner, you name it, it is probably here.

Among this bobbing mass of hulls and swaying masts is 'your' place, other crews watch your arrival critically always ready to take a line but brief and wary until they have your measure.

In a few days you will have integrated, become part of it all and feel as if you had never been anywhere else, friendships are formed, plans exchanged, help offered or declined, for everyone here has succumbed to a dream of some kind...

Many may have been here for ages, almost become settled; there's a joyful and enfolding camaraderie born of shared trials, shared dreams and experiences, some just get absorbed into the life and unwillingly leave, other voyagers are more seriously inclined; brains are picked, tools are borrowed, information exchanged, proposed voyages discussed and always the dream spurs you on.

Dreams vary; here's a man just retired on a small pension, his boat is his home, he seeks sun, sailing, and a new freedom after raising a family, he lost his wife last year, now he's looking for a new life.

This one has a drink problem; he knows it and isn't

ashamed of it but seeks to indulge it where the sun is warm and booze cheap. He's well liked, everyone looks after him, when people move somewhere else he gets ferried along with them. He's part of the scene, if he comes home staggering there's always someone to make sure he doesn't hurt himself or fall in, and who will see him safely tucked up for the night.

Another couple have sunk their all into their boat so they can have a taste of freedom before settling down into parenthood, they are young, enthusiastic, determined, perhaps if they are lucky they will follow their dream for a time and not settle too early. Once experienced this way of life can become like a drug; you always want the next fix, a dream to cling to.

Here is a delivery skipper keen to make a fast passage after he's restocked here, he'll be off in a day or so and perhaps he dreams that one day the boat he is on will be his own.

An elderly couple have arrived; they are a legend among sailing folk. They have been around the world three times already and will probably do so again. They're quiet and modest, competent yet a source of rich advice and anecdote, they don't see that they have done very much, yet when he retired they chose to have a boat built, live aboard her and set out on their voyages. They have no regrets, they write books of their travels but they don't have adventures; he says an adventure is usually the result of something you hadn't thought out properly or one of Mother Nature's little surprises!

But even in them the dream is still strong, the next corner waiting...

This is a transient and sometimes turbid community; it is as if one's street neighbours suddenly upped and vanished or new people move in coming out of the night to briefly be part of the scenery before disappearing again.

Time is not master of this village, the inhabitants bend it, use it, there's talk of work still to be done, stores to be laid in, of having to be in the right place to take advantage of winds and currents, there's talk of weather systems and routes to be taken, talk of old friends and their boats, peoples met with, sea lore, and always again and again the weather and the prospects for this or that passage yet to be made.

When the day's work is done they forgather on someone's boat or the jetty itself sitting out under the stars yarning and sharing a drink; wine oils tongues and memories and the talk ranges far and wide, narrow squeaks, balmy tropic days in the trade winds, storms and calms, voyages planned and voyages past, danger overcome, friends lost, the sound and thrust of the restless sea lies behind every word.

Each has broken away from the ties of the land for this period, they have joined with the ancient explorers, the merchant adventurers who created lands and fortunes, who paid the price at times in lives yet would not have done anything else for this is an ancient enchantment bewitching special people.

You listen, join in, immersed in what you are hearing but deeply aware of the sounds around you, for this life hones awareness and reaction, and you look out for each other; but you also want to learn in this school of experience and anecdote, for one day such knowledge could save your boat and your life. At the very least it provides you with information.

'Lovely little market there on a Friday everything cheap and good...'

'Talk to Ted, he's been there and says the entrance is easy once you clear the outer coral reef'.

'...had to reef right down and trail wraps astern... Dodgy business, three days of it we were glad to see it clear I can tell you...Seas breaking into the cockpit...'

'Shroud let go right in the middle and had to jury rig it with a halyard set up on the winch... All that heaving around I guess...nasty business'

'Not this year we left it too late so we're staying around till autumn, Greece and Turkey- maybe Cyprus if it's quiet, there's a new Marina in the Lebanon near Beirut... Jounieh... good but pricy, they went there last year.....'

'Val dropped a spanner over and we had to dive for it... Might try Ischia, or further south this year... cross next spring, Antigua looks nice...'

'Venezuela too... fabulous sailing but the authorities can

be a bit unpredictable outside Caracas...'

And so it goes, talk spiralling across voyages and seas, the stuff of exchange in a sailing community, each listener intent on pursuing the collective dream.

Boats arrive and depart, spurring you on to hurry your own departure; newcomers become familiar friends. You know all about them then one morning you open the hatch and they've gone, their empty space mocks you as you get ready for another day's work, You feel a sense of loss – pain even – looking out towards Tarifa you may spy a tiny white triangle... they are on their way.

Suddenly it's your turn, the moment steals up on you, one day there's a list of jobs to be done, repairs to be finished, stores bought, tanks filled, engine checked, gear gone over carefully and suddenly there are no more excuses, everything is done. You hardly dare speak of it, for goodbyes bring ill fortune. No, better slip out at dawn, all's well, let's be off.... Lines are retrieved quietly, the motor throbs and you slide away from the moorings, sails go up flapping idly till you clear the breakwater, then fill, hull and rigging creak, the boat heels to the breeze, the journey has begun.

By nine the Rock is fading astern, you wonder when and if you will see it again; briefly you remember those you have left, waking up to find that you too have gone. The reality is here and now, the dream has come alive. Gibraltar has played its part, and becomes just another memory... but there were corners."

Hawkish faces flecked with beads of sweat grinned in gap-toothed delight as a barely covered bosom gyrated above them, gnarled fingers coaxed wailing discords from a wide mouthed species of trumpet and we foreigners tried to blend in with the locals as best we could. Meanwhile the bride seemed completely out of it stoned to the wide on kif, kat or whatever... her participation in any ongoing activity looking increasingly doubtful.

A Moroccan wedding in the Casbah of Tangiers doesn't feature much in the average tourist itinerary and our own presence at this one was fortuitous.

Living and working on the Rock one winter we had come to be part of its small visiting community, our boat based in the newly opened Sheppards Marina.

Here, living aboard our boat we'd made friends with our neighbours on an ageing motor yacht and among their particular friends was Abdul.

Gibraltar's economy was growing, building and renovation work was going on apace; there was always a need for labour and Morocco provided it, many of its craftsmen and labourers coming over on the ferries to find work where wages were good and they could live away from home restrictions for a while. It also meant that they could save money; many like Abdul could then afford to marry.

Abdul worked on a building site with Tony our neighbour and was a frequent visitor to their boat, so it was natural that we met him; we liked him and he us so we were included when he invited Tony and his police-sergeant wife to the wedding.

There was another reason: Tony had offered to take Abdul over to Tangiers on his motorboat; the only trouble was that Tony understood little about sea crossings and knowing we did, had bashfully asked us to skipper his aged vessel on the journey.

Came the day and Abdul duly arrived carrying a large television set in a big box and accompanied by two other guests who were coming over with us, a dapper middle-aged Scot in a doeskin jacket and knife-edged cream trousers, beside him trotted a confection of wedge heels garish makeup and beehive hairdo called Rhoda.

Both of them promptly began emptying a bottle of scotch between them as we set out. It was a rough crossing. The strait has a habit of kicking up a wind over current chop that can test the strongest stomach. Abdul began to be ill over the stern, and we watched with interest as the dapper gent and Rhoda started their second bottle. However, Rhoda proved to be made of sterner stuff than we had supposed, telling us how she had been brought up helping her father on his fishing boat in the Hebrides and wasn't this a grand day... round one to Rhoda and whisky!

Things were fine to begin with until we eased out from the lee of Gibraltar's Rock into a 'sprackling-irritable' and uneven sea. Butting bows first into it, bits soon began to fall off the boat, the stem-head fitting disappeared, followed by a fairlead and part of a toe-rail and it was as well we got into the shelter of the land when we did or we might have lost more. Evidently Tony's boat needed something more than paint and varnish...

Tangier was a welcome relief. Abdul shot off ashore as soon as we berthed, two of his relatives scuttling ashore with the TV set between them before customs and port authorities could arrive.

The wedding was not for another day, and Abdul's family had arranged a side trip for us into the hills to visit other relations who had a farm up there. We were collected next morning by an aged VW van, which, together with another of its ilk was to be our transport for the journey.

Age had wearied it, the years had almost condemned. It staggered along belching smoke, rattling fit to fall apart, and, as we drove out of the city heavy rain began to fall. The VW began to climb up winding roads into the hills and its steering became more and more erratic, our driver wrenching his wheel over and waiting for the linkage to catch up, before heaving it over the other way. As our route was beset with steep drops here and there on both sides we were drained emotionally long ere we reached our destination...

Our hosts in true Moroccan fashion had been more than generous, a sumptuous meal awaited us once we had enjoyed our welcoming mint tea. Great trays of rice, chicken and mutton, with vegetables piled high awaited our pleasure. We ate heartily, seated on rugs, observing the custom of eating with the right hand only and mindful that much of this largesse would be needed later to feed the family.

Someone asked about a loo and others wanted the same facility so we were taken into the yard where a lean-to barn was possessed of a crude 'A la Turque' hole-in-the-ground surrounded by black plastic sheeting. It was very gloomy and one had difficulty in coming to terms with what one was trying to achieve but we managed and on emerging were charmingly met by a young boy with a basin of water and a grubby towel over his arm. I believe by local custom we were honoured; later we saw the washing up being done behind the house in an old metal wheelbarrow, practical solution to a common problem where there was no sink or piped water.

Our hosts sent us off at last with many good wishes and we knew why. The trip back to town was even more scary, as by this time the rain had turned the road to mud and we slid and skidded back down on balding tyres to a suburb where another family member welcomed us, with yet more food.... Hospitality in excess. Most of us were far too full to eat again but politeness said we must and badly distended we finally sagged wearily back on board the boat to sleep it all off.

Tapas bars abounded, so to one of these we went next morning for strong coffee and to get our instructions for the afternoon's events. Abdul had recovered from his sickness and took us round the Casbah showing us where we would be going and introducing us to all his merchant friends, One budding future seller, seven years old, kept tugging at our hand and saying "Very good my father's shop, Marks and Spencer, good prices! You come?"

The 'furnishing party' had already taken place readying the bride's new home and the 'Henna' party had been last night, so everything was 'Go' when we arrived. Musicians had been hired, along with belly dancers to keep the guests entertained; despite strict rules, alcohol it seemed, would be available to selected guests out of sight up on the rooftop.

Food was provided and everyone would be wearing their best for the occasion. At five pm we were told that the bride was on her way, and the groom with his retinue went off to meet them. The bride on her arrival seemed vacant... as one member of our party suggested, "If I was on duty in Gib I'd be detaining her for substance abuse..." and indeed she did seem to be rather heavily drugged.

The belly dancers were going round the room gyrating in time to the frantic music and thrusting large bosoms towards the guests who obligingly stuffed cash notes into their tops with wide grins. We were allowed to contribute and were expected to be generous; meanwhile the men had gone up to the roof accompanied by the police chief and were getting happy; now and then one trickled down to sway around the room, before puddling onto the floor, but they were soon back upstairs and most of the guests were high on kif which was freely circulating. Eventually we decided to go before things developed further; something was almost certain to happen and we didn't want to be there when it did!

The following morning we sailed in a flat calm back to Gibraltar accompanied by some cheerful dolphins, a lot of oranges and toilet rolls, and spare gas bottles, these things being in short supply at the time on the Rock. Everyone was expected to smuggle these necessities when they went 'over there'. It was one of Gibraltar's perennial disadvantages, this shortage of essentials, everything was either 'on order' or 'on a ship coming in soon'. Needless to say they seldom ever arrived!

Abdul however, turned up two weeks later very satisfied with his wedding shindig and sporting several bruises. We never asked whether they were from friends or his new wife but he appeared to be more than satisfied!

Chapter 12

Here and There

We have lived in some odd places. Now and again as we travelled we would settle for a time; usually these occasions were precipitated by a chance encounter, and the Forest of Dean was one such.

We had been down in the valleys above Swansea, looking, as always, for interesting properties, and it was on one of the return trips that we turned up the Wye valley to visit Tintern Abbey, and from there rather than retracing our route we drove instead towards Coleford and the road cutting across the Forest back to Gloucester and the M40.

Stopping in Cinderford for a rest we bought a paper and an 'Exchange and Mart' and began looking through the properties.

All at once Jan gave a yelp "What about this then? Semi-detached cottage part of a small group with land adjoining, no vehicular access, but good situation. Private sale and it's just around here somewhere"

We were hooked. Enquiry said it lay at the end of a track within the forest boundary. It had been a stable for the nearby quarry and had an overgrown quarry of its own as a garden.

Getting to it wasn't easy, we discovered that we must climb the side of the hill up wooden framed steps with gravelled treads, then make our way along the line of a hedge and dive through into a cement pathway which led down to yet more steps and a steep slope down to the cottage itself. All this was very overgrown but a small courtyard area faced onto an extension which formed the kitchen and an L shaped area between the house next door, and this.

The berserk barking of several dogs there warned us to stay clear, but the owner silenced them and told us that we could go and have a look, he would lend us the key.

Inside it felt decidedly damp. The lower back room was built underground and had no windows but the small sitting room seemed to have a cosy feel to it and a wood stove would soon dry it out.

The view from its window was across a valley to an ancient tree etched in palsied outline against a backdrop of pinewood; at the valley foot lay another small farm, beyond lay only sky.

Amid the overgrowth outside was a tumbledown privy, and a ruined pigsty ruled the lower slope of the steep walled garden. Behind the privy a sandstone cliff tufted with sparse growths reared to a ramshackle fence and orchard trees peering demurely above.

Climbing the garden we discovered an ancient wood bench lost among the grasses and from it one could look far out across Cotswold and the Severn River valley with glimpses of Gloucester and distant Cheltenham nestling just round the corner.

The deeply creased valley lying in between had another farm; a pine clad hillside shoulder limned the nearer fringe, a view to conjure with and a magically unexpected corner to occupy for a time...

Needless to say we bought it soon afterwards.

Jan was working in London so it became my business to renovate our new home. I quickly discovered 'Foresters' the folk of the Forest of Dean: anarchic, insular, proud of their old traditions and the history surrounding them, good friends, bad enemies, with a cynical and resigned view of life. I grew to respect and love them for their independent attitudes and cheerful good humour.

If you had been born in the Dilke – the local hospital – you were a true Forester. Old Dick informed me of this as we walked the dogs one day along the forest track. He and his brother shared a ruinous cottage down in the valley bottom and every evening they'd climb the steep and sometimes muddy slope leading to the pub. They were noted for their cider, created lovingly in the ramshackle shed alongside their cottage, and rumoured to contain much more than mere fermenting apple juices! Even a dead rat might find its way into the brew from time to time, and it was certain that pieces of meat were dropped in. Their cider was notorious, and rumoured to rob you of your mobility long before your brain, so that you were still able to appreciate your problem even while your legs belonged to somebody else and refused to support you!

There were other curiosities. Walking in the Forest around our new home one was likely to come upon occasional individuals loitering, as the term is…. Early cartoons often had hands-in-pockets characters whistling Dixie whilst 'hanging about', waiting until you had gone before resuming their depredations.

Here we discovered the same phenomenon; one simply did not ask!

Sheep formed a permanent backdrop to our new home, and they had 'rights'. It was nothing to find them ogling themselves in the wing mirrors and hubcaps of parked cars, slouching on pavements and kerbsides spattering raddle liberally all over, and enjoying freedoms such as marching up the high street with all the aplomb of parading aldermen or lying across roads to the inconvenience of passing traffic. Their owners seemed oblivious to inconvenience to the public and 'badgering' them, as the term was, only when it was necessary to shear, dip, or treat ailments. For much of the time they roamed freely and were only gathered when these indignities might be demanded of them; for the rest it was 'liberty hall' and they traded on their old rights in full measure.

It was another of the Forest's 'oddities'.

Carving out the overgrown garden we discovered old walls, a large vegetable garden which had evidently benefited from the pigsties beside it, since they were the most fecund and productive I have ever seen, and as we cleared area after area we began to find that beneath the chaos lay the foundations of a nice garden, someone had worked hard to wrest it from the stubborn rock.

Gradually we brought order of our own; we rebuilt the ruined piggeries into a tasteful two-tiered studio/workshop complex, put in paths, log stores, coal bunker, and steps to access them, tanked the underground room and brought it some light by means of a sloping ditch which pierced the wall via a glazed opening, installed a wood-burning stove, which as we had foreseen soon began drying out the property; we bridged the wide ditch around the house and put double doors from the bedroom onto the back lawn area, and a useful outhouse area from what had been a rubbish-filled annex.

Over the next couple of years we created a tasteful range of plantings to grace our quarry, grew to appreciate the old Roman mineshafts at the top end of the plot which were home to many bats, and insinuated ourselves into the locality.

The group of cottages had a communal aspect in that we all helped each other. Reliable water had always been a problem due to ancient pipes and practices, so we got together to re-pipe supplies though new systems, digging out the extensive trenches, and laying new pipes to all four houses. Paths were cleared and tracks maintained, everyone benefited.

Across the forest could be found ancient mines and lime kilns telling the ages old story of the forest's working life, from its earliest days when the Romans prospected here for lead and lime, charcoal in large quantities was produced later in the forest history to serve blast furnaces, and Forest of Dean coal was mined, many of the mines being 'free mines' when a forester who had the right to do so, would open up a private shaft or 'drift'

This right belonged only to those born within the Hundred of St Briavels and was regulated by local tradition in the miners' court.

The Hundred of St Briavels was taken to mean the whole area of the forest and applied to men of twenty-one years and more who had worked in a coal or iron mine for a year and a day; they were then deemed to be Free miners. They could start a mine anywhere in the forest as long as it was not under churchyards, gardens or orchards.

As a result there were mines and remains of them scattered all across the forest, even now walking there one suddenly comes across rusting tram lines, the coal carts, or a gaping hole in the forest floor. Most have been fenced but there is still danger, one walks with care, and aware of possibilities...

The closure of the Dilke Hospital, and commercial considerations mean that there are relatively few free miners left, a few struggle on and by exploiting tourism and local opportunities keep a precarious living going but new laws and new generations are against their survival and it will not be long before another traditional occupation is lost there.

At the top of our hill track was a red phone box. Ordinarily it was a pleasant walk with the dogs to go up to make your call, and until we got a phone of our own it was our only way of contacting the outside world.

In summer it could be a joy. In winter it became a scrabbling struggle up a frosty macadam track and finger-numbing minutes spent trying to look up the number one wanted or skating back down the hill when you had run out of coins.

One early spring Sunday afternoon as we took the dogs up the hill for their stroll we were at once struck by several figures grouped around the box; evidently something was amiss.

Reaching them we asked if we might help in any way, The telephone book tatty at the best of times had completely disappeared and it seemed they were trying to get in contact with some local garage to come and rescue their broken-down car, They were a Birmingham family down for the day, five of them including parents and grandparents and their car had faded out just up the lane.

We invited them home to use our phone and our book and give them a restorative cup of tea for they were weary and dispirited.

We found a garage, cheered them up and were glad when the mechanic came out and managed to get their car going, off they went. But soon they returned, bringing us gifts of thanks and a friendship began which over time blossomed into a very happy relationship for us all.

The grandparents proved to be marvels at house-sitting, and on several occasions cared for our home while we were away abroad, looking after the dogs and keeping house and garden immaculate, doing many small jobs which more than aided us. We are friends to this day.

It was just one of the many surprises that made living in the forest such a joy for us, and enriched our lives so greatly.

Surrounding the forest lay many small villages, each with its own history. Those along the line of the River Severn had been small ports from which 'trows', the small coasting barges of the Bristol channel, had carried away the forest's coal, charcoal, iron ore and stone from Blakeney and Newnham, Lydney, and small wooden jetties along the river.

Some of it went to Wales, some across to Bristol and the ports of Somerset, much went upriver to fuel the furnaces where iron making was beginning to become a serious business, with the railways and iron ships evolving. In addition there were potteries and it's not too hard to see how such forests also provided timber for shipbuilding 'crucks' and hammer-beams for manors and churches, wood for building jetties, and of course pit props which in the Welsh mines would have been much wanted.

Indeed even at the bottom of our own bit of valley there were old lime kilns, and lead mines long abandoned to bats and decay, while just at the top of our quarry garden were two deep dark drifts which some said were Roman. History and the raw materials which fuelled it were all around.

Nearby too were great ponds, reservoirs for mills and workshops, and these falling into disuse had hedged themselves around with matted undergrowth and now, with track ways put in, provided us with lovely dog walks.

Climbing to the top of one hill you might look down upon Severn vale and the sinuous river making its way through fields and copses, a once vibrant highway for trade. It was no rare thing in medieval times to find quite large barges making their way up to Shrewsbury and beyond, for the seasonal fairs; wool too, from the Welsh marches, and fat bales from the rich border lands hemming the Welsh lands on the English side.

The forest had seen them all come and go, years of plenty, years of want; forest life had been forged from hardship, the foresters' independent characters had been moulded by adversity and induced a sublime dislike of regulation. Foresters were turbulent and at times unruly and more than once troops had been sent in to enforce regulations and quell disturbances.

As one Forester told me "We'm a funny lot, we either likes thee or we dun't...." I was blessed to find that mostly they 'did'.

When we left it was with the deep regret of leaving what had become to us 'family' and while the next corner beckoned, it was hard to turn one's back on the last one.

It had never occurred to us that we might live on Kent's strange Dungeness peninsula. Previous encounters had almost always been from the perspective of a heaving yacht's deck. Whichever way you approached it the bleak shingle banks stretched away in either direction, and a landmark block of gaunt square buildings rising slowly from the sea taking, it seemed, forever to reach and forever to leave, astern only gradually revealing reluctant shorelines emerging from its frequent haze, impersonal and lacking all attraction.

Almost inevitably it would be passed in the chill grey of a dawn after a cold night on deck, or bleary-eyed coming up on watch and seeing its gaunt form emerging from the undulating pewter carpet of the English Channel. Slowly one crawled towards it, then abruptly for a brief instant one seemed uncomfortably close to the shingle beach, its offshore dolphin marking an outfall pipe and either sweeping astern rapidly on a fair tide or painfully gained, its fringe of chilled and petrified anglers poised between hope and despair, and a scrawny line of fishing boats hauled out high on its steep shingle rim while a few desultory cottages straggled away into misty infinity along groin-etched flanks.

Power lines snaked away into distance pendant on Orwellian pylons striding unstoppably across the landscape conjoined by pendant wires and by other pylons and vanishing into distance, a few jets of steam or occasional lighting often the only indication that the place was in use.

A striped lighthouse peered hopelessly from its inland site

together with a more modern erection but the overall impression was that one passed the place with relief for it offered neither comfort nor shelter.

With such memories nothing could have prepared us for our eventual move there. Life has a habit of producing the unexpected and circumstances forced us to sell our remote Forest of Dean cottage. Moving back to central London with two country-raised dogs was clearly unacceptable; we began to look for alternatives. Surrey was way outside our budget and it was Ashford with its quick rail service to London that decided us to look around New Romney as a natural option. Sea, sand, open spaces, somewhere to live for a time, and still breathe.

Perhaps we should not have come to enjoy the area quite so much if we hadn't got lost on our first trip there.

Goodness knows where we went wrong, but we found ourselves in a great flat expanse bisected by twisting lanes, streams and drains, dotted with perfunctory clumps of copse and spinney lines of reed, occasional isolated tiny churches swimming in flat seas of greenery and long views of sameness broken only by the occasional spire or the block outlines of the distant Dungeness power station.

Romney Marsh has many facets, best known among them its reputation as the one-time haunt of smugglers. Kipling wrote his 'Smugglers' poem about this area: "Five and twenty ponies trotting through the dark…" etc. and the 'Dr Syn' books were based around fabled characters in the locality.

Indeed on a foggy day here you might easily believe in almost any old tale as the marsh enfolds you in its strangeness.

Many of the old churches out on the marshes had the reputation of being caches for smuggled goods and outlying farms might very well provide Kipling's 'Woodpiles', villages wild, sparsely-inhabited, deeply insular and even today you may see in the faces of the fishermen that same reckless spirit lurking that might chance anything heedless of consequence…

Into this odd corner we found ourselves suddenly tipped. It was raining, a chill mist arose from the marshes and the tower of a distant church seemed to beckon then was gone again, as we drove narrow winding lanes among screens of bushes, reed-fringed canals with scattered farms dotted across a fragmented landscape, and ethereal glimpses of a sameness which defied map reading.

We stopped at one tiny church trying to locate ourselves. It lay in the middle of a meadow surrounded by ditches. Going inside as we later did was to discover immense peace; the beauty of timelessness an ongoing simplicity so lacking elsewhere.

That same simplicity was woven into the very fabric of this silent building; its several 'boxes' spoke of ancient family connections, whilst the isolation and evident seasonal flooding meant that it was intimate with its landscape. Later we found others, one with its bell tower sat beside it on the ground, contemptuous of convention and enfolded in its own character which defied all regulation. Inside again one found that same great peace.

A few lights sparkled fitfully through the mists, and suddenly we were back in the world of cottages and small shops and our bed and breakfast destination close at hand.

Such an early encounter fascinates. We found ourselves wanting to see more, experience this curious time-warp world and become familiar with its charms and pitfalls... Another corner was opening out before us. We wanted to look around it.

It can be disconcerting to one accustomed to more conventional places to discover one's new home sitting on a pad of concrete in the midst of a sea of shingle.

True, concrete roads linked you with the outer world but your garden was laid in shingle, your surroundings were largely the same stuff overlaid by a very thin veneer of patchy soil and introduced plant life clinging tenaciously to its unstable bed.

Critical minds might cringe at the very idea, but we had not lived there for long before we began to appreciate other aspects to this seeming blasted heath of pebbles.

For one thing in springtime it blossomed into fragile and vibrant beauty. Along the margins of the sea the shingle erupted into flower, Valerian in great drifts, sea grass, sea holly, evening primrose, poppy in great swathes on empty lots, and vetch, spread a fragrant blanket across the expanses. Among the scant turf covering grew miniature ragged robin, sedums, buttercup and a thorny scrub which lent form and broke up the fractured rubble of old concrete emplacements and moribund railway sleepers buried deep in a gravelled bed.

Foxes' earths drilled dark holes in sandy dunes flecked with sparse wispy grass in clumps and vestigial rickety chestnut fencing linked by twisted strands of rusting wire, barrier to nothing more than imagination. Along the sea's margin the beach extended, half a mile wide at neap tides, stretching away into distance as it curved towards Dymchurch and Hythe and confined by solid sea walls of sculpted concrete.

Most of the time this vast area of beach was deserted. In high summer tourists came but most of the year it lay pristine save for a few fishermen pegging their nets for flatfish.

This transient world gave rise to its own characteristic features, the line of boats hauled along the front at Littlestone, the thickening band of houses fringing the shingle and its road, while down along the area of shingle spit behind the power station lay a small community of fisher folk, holiday cottages, hauled boats, and a couple of pubs together with gardens created largely from the washed-up detritus of the shoreline.

Odd shaped pieces of wood, lobster creels, red and yellow and orange plastic buoys and net floats, coloured rope, stones with holes in them, all were turned into garden ornaments which, together with a few 'created' flower-beds and some native species, turned plebeian shingle garden areas into lively and interesting features ably complementing the clapboard shacks and old railway carriage cottages.

These had once predominated, hauled here as holiday homes, and even though built upon, their origins were still clear even though much altered.

Through all this ran the railway. The Romney Hythe and Dymchurch railway still runs its fleet of delightful steam locomotives and carriages in scheduled services which began between the wars, were a part of the defences of the area throughout the second war and continue operating to the present day.

Indeed, one of the frequent punctuation marks in a day is the sound of the trains passing, together with the scents of hot oil and coal smoke as the little engines thunder along their track, the carriages full of tourists while others wait eagerly at flashing road crossings to catch a glimpse or get a photo of a classic mini steam engine. At the café beside the lighthouse they can get up close and personal with these wonderful little trains, bearing their loads of tourists between Hythe, Dymchurch, New Romney and the lighthouse and café. In between times they ferry schoolchildren. Railway and marsh seem inseparable, in peace and wartime they have been mutually supportive, and to spend a day without the sound of one of the engines hustling along was to know dearth, a piece missing from marsh life.

Along the line of the coast just inland lie a series of gravel pits. These now form an active bird reserve. Migrants on their journeys pause here often and it is an area well beloved by 'twitchers' laden with binoculars and cameras. Once again the marsh surprises and it's a not uncommon thing to find rarities among the avian visitors as well as one or two eccentrics among the twitchers who later gorge themselves on fish and chip lunches in the pubs and depart, replete in all respects and very happy.

Down here close to the power station one might suppose that nothing good could happen. The cooling ponds, it's true, create habitats for some marsh birds, a few swans in season and their reed-fringed margins give a semblance of natural beauty. At one time a railway track cut through from the main line, long disused save in the memories of a few older people; its abandoned route soon overgrew.

Sleepers rotted away into the turf, rabbits burrowed beneath them and under the bristling blackthorn lining the way, foxes sculpted old concrete bases, digging deep beneath, and the spoil they threw up, along with that of the rabbits was soon covered in the miniature plant life which abounds across this fragile landscape.

At one time a small miracle took place here, and I know of it because I saw it, and for a time was a part of it.

A local artist began making elaborate creations out of cement and resin and amongst his pieces were lovely little cottages each fantastically decorated with a myriad treasures for which he scoured markets and rubbish tips. He made them not for sale but to please himself and his cottages became wondrous confections studded with marbles, coloured stones, old jewellery, watches, mirrors, earrings, stones with holes in them, bottle tops, glowing beads, flashing bright glass ovals in dozens of colours; and when he finished a piece he would sometimes take it to a special place placing it beneath a bush beside a lake; he planted flowers around it, small figures of glass and ceramic, little chairs and tables, anything his fancy fixed upon.

One of these cottages was put here beside the mere, among the reeds and bushes, we watched and cared for it and for a time it was clear that others had seen the small miracle and added things of their own, more flowers, a glass owl, a couple of small deer, a golliwog figure, a bear...

Clearly his magic had touched other souls, dog walkers and strollers who, like ourselves enjoyed this odd landscape; for a while the little corner glowed with wondrous joy and resonated with its charm in so unlikely a setting.

But as with all dreams the crass foolishness of man intervened. Overnight a group of youths found, and used the setting for target practice hurling stones at it, smashing its baubles, wrenching the remains of the jewelled cottage from its bed, trampling the flowers, stealing the little figures, wantonly destroying what had given pleasure to so many.

The Angels only come to such places once, No new cottage was ever put in its place and we lost something of beauty and something of ourselves too... But the memory persists, the little corner still lives in certain minds...

...Along with a sadness that wanton savagery still exists among us. But that's another story.

Among the fishermen's cottages down on the tip of Dungeness, that created by Derek Jarman needs mention.

Many will already be familiar with how he came here in the later years of his life to a timber cottage and how he created an amazing garden from the flotsam washed up on the beaches and collected day by day on his walks, and by using salt-tolerant local plants with a few imported shrubs he made a living jewel in this unlikely place. Jarman was a film maker, an author and painter, a unique mind, and good friend to many. He throve on Dungeness, it seemed to have enfolded him as it does so many, he became part of its iconic curiosity. Here on this wind-seared tip he brought life and beauty, and left an undying legacy.

We spent three very happy years amid this strange environment, always finding something new, thriving on the long beach walks. Like Jarman I collected washed up pieces from our own part of the beach, my front garden was full of odd-shaped lobster pots, strange bits of sea-washed wood, coloured floats, net corks, and a myriad treasures brought home, and I learned to love the delicious mornings before the sun rose, when the sea was a misty expanse, the sun illumining it in golden splendour, or lifting from the horizon in vivid scarlet and orange glows.

The line of sand dunes fringes the beach, vibrant with gorse and yellow poppy, skylarks sang in the profound blue overhead and sometimes waves sighed and surged among the shingle, or their sound formed a backdrop to the dawn, and the cries of gulls and waders along the sea's hissing rim.

Beauty lies in the eyes and mind of the beholder, I wrote a poem to celebrate these mornings.

Five in the morning- the sea is black-
Sighing on beach or clattering shingle,
Dogs root in dunes- won't go back-
Or leave until dawn and ocean mingle,
Rusty reds appear- the footlights glow-
Cloudy curtains part to bare a stage,
Of sky and sea, the sun begins his show-
Ushers in new day- soon new age,
Red, gold blue the costumes daze-

Senses, thrilled by windborne scent,
Of night-weary Fox- the seaward haze-
Draws the curtain down- the play is spent.

Surrounding the marsh lie its satellite villages- Lydd,
Appledore, Newchurch, Ham Street, Brookland, St Mary
in the Marsh, and many more both existent and lost.

Each possesses something of the richness of the area, its
history, its uniqueness, and just on the fringes are others,
Winchelsea, and especially, Rye.

The latter provides a veritable cornucopia of delights with
its narrow streets, its delightful shops, its half-timbered
cottages and inns, and crowning the hill, its lovely church
dominant; one of my own favourite things in this lovely place
is a small and silent chapel beside the Franciscan Friary down
a cottage-lined and flowery street.

There lit by sunlight pouring in through a lovely solar is as
quiet a place as you may find anywhere in our crowded
country; its silence is profound, and happy are they who
discover it on their own and go inside just to sit amid the quiet,
a small refuge still, in a big world.

Tourists are beginning to find these places. It is a sad fact
that the places we cherish most become the most eagerly
sought and at once lose their charms. Too many people seeking
too little of such quiet, happily many still want the shops and
pubs, the arcades and alleys; one can still find peace if you
really look for it.

The Harbour itself lies at the junction of three rivers,
originally the main river, the Rother, ran to sea at New
Romney but horrendous storms in the thirteenth century
changed the river's course and combined with erosion from the
seaward side, so changed things that Rye became one of the
best of the Cinque Ports.

It was also home to smugglers, primarily of wool, and was
notorious for the violent 'Hawkhurst' gang who met at the
Mermaid Inn; Isolation, scattered small communities, the
lonely nature of the marsh and its reputation as a strange
region of will-o-the-wisp spectres, marsh gas and insular

inhabitants all combined to defy forces of the law for some years.

Fishing has always been one of the prime employments around the region. In the past stake nets were put up and stretched out from the beaches at given times, the men who served them summoned by flags, and having to cross the shingle wearing 'pattens', a type of snowshoe made especially for the purpose, and the boats of today drawn up and launched by winches from steep shingle banks. There are families whose living still depends upon them, among them several whose shops sell fresh fish caught or brought in daily and make delightful places to visit and buy one's tea.

Small delicious fresh shrimps and prawns vie with Dover soles, plaice, cod, whiting, cockles and mussels, eels, and fresh samphire in season to provide a delight, and if that were not enough The Pilot just across the road, together with the Britannia beside the lighthouse each serve fish and chip lunches to die for! And Dungie 'mud' puddings.

In summer tourists try their hand in the shallows and more serious locals can be seen carrying the wide shrimping nets favoured in these parts, while low tide will often see someone staking flounder nets out across the beach margins in the early mornings.

Of course at times there are drawbacks: blown sand borne on high sea winds, sifting across roads and gardens, and shingle and more shingle but as with so many things, adaptation and compromise blunt their impact and I know very few residents who don't vigorously defend this strange place if it is criticised or threatened.

Rightly so. Life needs its contrasts, walking the dogs across the wide mossy expanses, finding miniature wildflowers hidden among the brambles, with a fresh breeze, clean and wholesome blowing in your face, is to know the freedom of those who have always made Dungeness their home and gives a sense of something very close to love for this odd corner of England.

Chapter 13

'Secluded Location'

Once again life's turning seasons saw us thinking of new things. Jan was not happy in our seaside home and the end of her working life was looming. She felt she wanted to move, and we started to plan for the day of her retirement, putting the house on the market and getting the van ready for an extended journey.

I am often asked why we decided to go and live in France in the first place. I might answer in Dickensian fashion 'Dogs Sir!

At that time one had to make a choice, England had quarantine regulations which meant that your extended family, if taken abroad, would on their return be incarcerated for six months in a kennel. The reason, rabies.

I am first to say that nobody would want that in the UK. Its potential is horrendous but it did mean decisions had to be made which might not otherwise have been necessary.

We had exhausted ourselves looking for a home in England. Jan retired at sixty and the day afterward we were in the motor home and away on a sweeping quest which took in most of the lower half of England.

Much of it we already knew, we'd lived in parts of it and over several years we had combined weekend travelling with looking at property. To begin with we had been ahead of the game, but as years passed we began to lose ground as house prices soared. Indeed we had gone through the same depressing experience in our sailing days, when the cost of keeping a boat became more and more prohibitive, moorings the same; the choices became fewer, eventually on both fronts, we had to give in.

This was our last fling.

We began in Somerset. Over the years we'd seen some

very attractive prospects down there and, living in the Forest of Dean as we had, it had been close enough to be explored at weekends.

There had been some interesting forays among its backroads.

Like this one: we were following up an advert in Exchange and Mart, which was our bible in those days. There was a cob cottage advertised, set in tranquil surroundings with no vehicle access but with its own piece of copse and heath behind. It also lay within our price range; we phoned and made an appointment to view....

It was an unusual place hard to locate and the owner's instructions had been curious "Find the track leading from the farm gate and follow it till you get to the heath, walk across that following the footpath – it's about half a mile – and you'll see the house down in the dip, Yes it has water, but not laid on to the house, no electric, only oil lamps or gas lanterns; there's a big range in the kitchen – but you'll see it all when you arrive....."

We followed instructions, a long walk on a wet day, the track streaming with water on all sides; as we crested the hill we saw that it was now all running downhill towards the cottage which had come into view. Nestled against a tall spindly copse a trickle of smoke appearing from its single chimney, the house had the appearance of leaning, its walls scabby and unloved, its thatched roof dangerously aged and the garden around it bare and saturated.

Still we had come to view it and the lady owner was pleasant, offering us tea, fetching the water from her weed covered open well. With tadpoles and bird droppings in mind we accepted hesitantly, but the resulting brew was one of the best we ever tasted.

We began to talk about the house, and now a curiosity arose; she would show us the downstairs only, saying she hadn't tidied up upstairs. Ok we thought, for the moment. As we sat in the sitting room we were aware of odd noises around us; she explained that cob 'settled' in damp weather. We glanced at each other suspicion in our eyes – but it was not this that aroused our curiosity – she would not talk of price. She told us that the land around was hers, that there was no chance of getting a road put across the moor, that the well never dried up (this we could believe!) and that it had been in her family for generations.

We were becoming aware of something else: she didn't want to sell it! Gradually she came to explain that it could be very lonely out here and so from time to time she would advertise her property and bring in a few people to talk to. Like us in fact!

Neither of us minded. In a way it seemed completely logical; if you wanted company you brought it to you rather than going out across the heath to find it. We found, looking into our hearts that we couldn't argue. So 'Why Not?'

We left after a very good walk, a lovely cuppa and a nice chat, happy that we had made someone else happy, and relieved that we would not have to make an offer for the tumbledown but much-loved dwelling.... The only thing is... we are curious still, for we wonder if the house is still standing after hearing all those 'Noises off!'

We tended to like the 'odd'. This included anything way out but this trip was pushing the boundaries a bit even for us.

Exmoor to those who don't know it can be bleak in the extreme, and today was one of 'those' days.

Guided by an estate agent's blurb we had made our way through sinuously winding lanes with wayside trees becoming more and more laden with Spanish moss and lichen, tokens as we knew, of pure air free of polluting substances, Very well but once again we found ourselves almost afloat.

The moor beside us was doing its best to flood the lane, and when we finally reached the track leading to the property we had come to see it was so deep in water that the dog had to swim in places.

Tirelessly and with good humour we trekked on following the line of a dry stone wall which was acting as a dam and guiding the gathered waters of the moor straight onto the property.

Wading knee-deep most of the time we explored this

'gem' as it was described, a single story erection naked inside, unappealing in its rotted timbers, green slimed floors and tumbled ruin alongside. Yet one could see possibilities: rebuild, plaster and tank the interior, new floor, roof, and doors and windows, a big hearth, even bottled gas heating might turn it from the derelict it was into something approaching a nice home.

Of course you would have no electricity, no telephone, no direct sanitation, no rubbish collection, but one could see its potential. Cosy oil lamps, put in a septic tank or natural recycling plant, compost everything you could. In the end you might even get a garden going.

On the minus side there would be a long haul to nearest village groceries, petrol station and communications. Further still in times of crisis as one got older, ambulances might find it a struggle as might carrying you out, post collection would involve a long walk down to the road, and 'wet-wet-wet' half the year, not much better even in summer as the moor drained down, it had no well, no neighbours, only deer and sheep for company and by now even the dog was shuddering, we were damp to the eyeballs and reluctantly we left this 'find' to someone else... but interesting? Definitely!

Another such, this time the 'gem' in truth and reality set high above Swansea on a hilltop at the edge of a small hamlet. As we drew up beside it a Red Indian tepee, evidently recently occupied, vied with the property itself which was a two storey cottage in fairly good repair and currently in use as stable and cattle byre.

Exploring further, its blessings began to manifest themselves. A rushing streamlet set in rocky landscape, a waterfall, three ponds, fresh running water from the hills; one could easily envision a waterwheel driving a generator. A pub lay just next door, a village with small shops only a couple of miles away, together with a petrol station. The whole lay on a hillside thus draining all rain back into the river. It possessed fertile slaty soil, and of course a tepee... All this was related to us by the pub landlady as we bought drinks and sandwiches for lunch.

It was owned at the time by a five-person commune who were it appeared, giving up life here in the wilderness – other pursuits called them – and the price seemed right; off we sped to the agent.

Here we discovered that the price had just gone up, our subsequent offers were twice gazumped and it rapidly drew away from our league as several other buyers vied to own it.

This was beginning to be a common experience; we sighed and went off to see a shoe-making concern and cottage in a town with one of those unpronounceable names – sounded to us like 'Mehuntleth' – but only a Welshman would know!

By error on leaving this place, we took a wrong turning and found ourselves on one of the most hair-raising tracks we had ever driven. Climbing steeply, it curved around the shoulder of a hillside poised high above a deep and gloomy valley, with a rushing stream running along its foot amid glacial boulders reminding one of the Khyber Pass. We eventually got out of it at the far end via a gate, but by then we were white and shaken, and most grateful for a drink at a handy pub, even though nobody wanted to speak English to us...

Wales was proving to be interesting if daunting and this was made amply clear when we went to look at a terraced house in a village on the Llyn Peninsular. Driving down its main street we were stridently aware of the silence, and curtains twitching in our wake; clearly one would never be alone! But then, who would ever want to live there anyway?

Further north as we moved upcountry, we looked around Lancashire, the Dales and Yorkshire Moors, before coming down to Lincolnshire and North Norfolk which had always felt like a second home. Even here we were being marginalized by rising prices and finally we had to give up after a visit to a friend in Suffolk, who had just paid for her new town home far more than we had got for our bungalow in Kent. As we covered these areas we grew more and more depressed; anything set in countryside or with a view was getting outside our remit, and the most affordable and best placed bungalow we found proved to be made of asbestos and needed rebuilding and would not qualify for a mortgage anyway.

At the end of five weeks we found ourselves ensconced on a Kent campsite, living permanently in our van; the house had been sold, the dogs were aboard, tickets had been booked on the Tunnel, it was time to bid England goodbye for a time and seek our fortune elsewhere.

Readers of my book 'The View From Here' will have followed our journey through France in search of a home. We never regretted the move. Sometimes when the wind blows it's better to bend with it...

You never know what you will encounter round the next corner. Sailing along the French coast one misty early morning in our old wooden Gaff rigged yacht we were surprised all at once to find ourselves in the middle of a naval fleet exercise.

All around lay warships large and small, as we sailed peacefully on, an urgent high speed launch surged alongside, its American commander almost apoplectic.

He demanded to know who we were and what the F....! we thought we were doing there.

Making a passage to our next port of call we told him. His fury knew no bounds "This is a restricted zone closed to shipping. A wireless warning went out yesterday and is being repeated every hour!"

We pointed out that we didn't have a radio.

"Jesus! What kind of boat are you? You don't even appear on our radar," he yelled "nobody can see you!"

We apologised; meanwhile a helicopter and a barge with a senior officer aboard circled us hungrily. By the looks we were getting it seemed likely that we'd be court martialled at the very least. We promised to go as quickly as we could, but the wind was light, the engine was playing up and we were in no hurry. We explained all this together with the fact that a wooden boat like ours seldom appeared on a radar; we had lost our reflector some time before and had not yet got the new one and it was not obligatory to carry one anyway in a boat our size, nor a radio either on small craft in those days, and we were not being dogmatic merely 'traditional'. It was they, we felt, who were playing the wrong game, not us.

I still wonder just what they put into their log to record the event. We were clear in half an hour, after which landing craft and more helicopters made the sea cacophonous with their discord behind us. It was very peaceful sailing along gently that morning, perhaps they should have tried it...

Peace comes in other forms too, I well remember the first time that I visited St Peter Port on the island of Guernsey. We had crossed from England in a smart trawler-type yacht; the island was one of the owner's favourite places, I soon discovered why.

You anchored in those days, in a wide 'pool' just inside the railway jetty. It was summer haven for a dozen or so visiting yachts. You went ashore in your dinghy, tying up at the outer end of the inner harbour mole or, if the tide was high, you could drop your passengers in the inner harbour close to the town.

This area was full of moored boats and dried-out at low water, it was ideal for going alongside the high stone wall and carefully drying out to scrub the boat's bottom of marine growth or put on an extra coat of paint. The chandler just across the road, Marquand's, supplied your every need and one dined up at the yacht club or in one of the little restaurants around town.

Every day, morning and afternoon one of the British Rail ferries from Weymouth would steam into the port and laboriously turn herself around to back into her berth, which was on the inside of the jetty. Both in arrival and departure a rope would be taken to the big buoy near the moorings, together with a courageous buoy jumper who waited to make fast or cast off, and the big ships would haul themselves in or out, the wire rope twanging alarmingly, while the buoy hand clung on for dear life; finally the vessel berthed or departed but for the moored yachts it could be a nervous moment as we all swung to our anchors, often fouling each other in the process. But nobody minded, it was part of the game.

St Peter Port itself was at that time a duty free port. You could buy many kinds of goods which were subject to customs duty in England, and visitors to the Channel Islands were allowed to buy a small quantity for personal use free of customs tariff, attraction enough in itself; but there were other joys and one of them at this time lay among Guernsey's wonderful markets.

Here you might wander happily along aisles lined with ice-laden slabs attractively laid out with displays of glowingly fresh shellfish in large varieties, mackerel fresh from the sea, bright eyed wrasse and pollock, codling, bream, bass, mullet and flatfish with many more. Nearby another section was given over to vegetables, especially the tomatoes for which Guernsey was famous, another given over to fruit, yet another to extravagant shows of flowers, in an atmosphere both lively and cheerful; or one might wander out and climb the narrow streets until you could look down on the port and on your own boat rocking gently at her mooring.

It was a place of sun and sea. I returned there often over the years in many different craft. But change was on the way, On the last occasion we were there with our own boat on our way south; the inner harbour had had a tidal barrier placed across its entrance, pontoons were being installed, a marina created, and they told us we would probably be one of the last boats to have a free berth while the work was completed. The changes affected many; the ferries Alouette and Silhouette could only come to its steps at high water and we lost a delightful venue to commercial considerations.

Of course it had to happen; yachting was booming, more and more boats wanting to come, many wanting to stay. Hydrofoils now used the main port, fishing was largely dying, cross channel trade in flowers and tomatoes was now being sent by air, the Commodore ships disappeared, and the very lack of infrastructure which had kept St Peter Port the tranquil haven it was to us had changed, and we had to change with it.

The ferries to Herm still ran. The 'Harpoon'- that odd-shaped, black-hulled new (then) arrival, probably still bounces her way out of harbour along with many more familiar names. The old 'Dame de Sark' no longer lies at the outer quay and yes, once again I'm nostalgic. I loved the place as it was when

I first discovered it and fished prawns under its railway pier, our teas were always exciting for we had caught them ourselves… but sadly the most potent of magic often lives only in our memories…

Down on the Southern tip of the island lies a bay. Here one can drop anchor and lie at peace under the cliffs facing a delightful small beach reached either by dinghy or by very steep steps, and part of a small silent corner seldom interrupted, ideal for doing those jobs of painting and varnishing well away from the blown dust of the quaysides in town.

Here one can swim in crystal-clear waters, catch limpets and mussels off the rocks, dive for lobsters along the rock edge, or listen to the mewing gulls and watch the scattering clouds of the mackerel shoals roiling among the tide rips beyond the point and mobbed by shrieking flocks of gannets or gulls.

Such places are becoming rare; the huge increase in boating sees most of them overwhelmed in time, their peace destroyed in the very search for it.

Guernsey – the Guernsey I first knew – has followed the same pattern, the harbour has grown beyond recognition. New marinas harbour more yachts, massed cars making parking impossible after eight in the morning and the market has become a shadow of itself, while air travel brings tourists in droves, and property prices go through the roof.

No… leave me my memories and the gentler days and ways that fill them.

But still I owe these islands homage, and wrote this poem anchored one day in the silence of that bay with just the sound of the wavelets lisping among the rocks.

Green are the Island's nearer shores-
The outer hooked like teeth or claws,
And swift tides run through shattered seas-
In racing currents that etch and tease-
the sharp fanged rocks-or careless caress,
sandy beaches- no force possess,

To tear and grind in the inner bays-
Where tourists spend the balmier days.
But far to the North, on up-flung piles-
The Casquets guard these Channel Isles,
While in the West, Les Hanois light-
With steel-gleam fingers probes the night,
Yet here in changing summer places-
Where hay fields stand above tide races-
Is where I often dream of being,
I close my eyes, my mind still seeing-
The silent bays, where anchored fast-
I knew such joy in times gone past,
The solitary watch in evening light
And the magic of a sea hawk's flight.

Nothing can re-capture such timeless quality; we search in vain for last year's 'rainbow' traces. Life moves on and our cherished places disappear one by one under the march of modernity.

But they live in us. They are never 'lost' as long as we go on recalling them.

Chapter 14

Motorhomes and Musings

Motor-homing is one way of seeing around that next corner. Our own experiences began in a small way with a combination unit of pick-up and a dismountable caravan body.

The fellow who had owned it had bought it as a gift to his wife; she had decided at once that she would use the pick-up but not the unit. It was dismounted and put into a barn still brand new.

That was where we were blessed, for we saw it advertised, we had just disposed of a caravan because our new home had no spare parking space but with this unit we would still take up the same space yet have a caravan as well; logical solution to a logical problem!

And so it turned out, When we went to see it we were astonished that it was available; nothing had been touched, it was a new van, with new furnishings, new bedding, everything pristine except the pick-up, which she had used a few times to go into Monmouth market; it too was almost new. With the caravan unit mounted we were now able to go down to the French barn, dismount the unit in the farmyard at the bottom of the track, live in it while we worked on the barn restoration, use the truck to fetch and carry, and pick the whole thing back up when we wanted to go home for a time. Everything was ok and we got along famously.

But lives move on and when we sold the barn we had to think again.

We'd always liked the look of the German Hymers, sleek and modern, spacious, beautifully and durably fitted out, they had seemed the acme of perfection when we'd first seen one; but they were outside our (then) price-range.

We compromised by buying a new Italian-made van.

Within a few months it was showing its age, with trim pieces falling off, badly sealed windows leaking, basins coming apart, services causing trouble. As ex boating people we were accustomed to things that were of good quality which not only worked but carried on working, so we were very unsatisfied with lesser products. The upshot was that we traded the van in and bought a second-hand Hymer anyway... and blow the expense!

Almost immediately we realised the wisdom of our choice. It was comfortable, well appointed, solid and reliable; for the next few years it did everything we asked of it and more. We took it all over France, England, Wales, Cornwall, Devon, and up to the Dales and Cumbria without any problem.

But our hearts still lay in France. By that time we were spending our winters down in Spain and Portugal; in prolonged periods of bad weather it began to be evident that we still needed a higher level of comfort. We were getting older, our needs changing, so when the time came to part with the van it was natural to look for another and larger Hymer.

An advert in one of the Motorhome magazines told of a company in Belgium who were selling these brand new ex-factory at very reasonable prices, we decided to go to see what they had.

There was only one choice: looking around their premises we saw many lovely vans but inside the showroom we discovered our dream vehicle.

It was as if we had suddenly come home... We had seen them before on sites down in Portugal and Spain; they had impressed us with their size and quality of fitting out and here, as we mounted its steps, lay our perfect van. True, it was rather large, but every frustration of space and comfort melted away in the face of this magnificent beast! It ticked every box. The only question was, could we afford such a van and could we drive it in the sort of confined spaces we often found ourselves in?

Its price amazed us, it cost us less than forty thousand pounds, a fraction of what a similar sized American RV would have been. As to its manoeuvrability we would just have to try.

The salesman was cautious if amiable when I suggested that I might drive it to the nearest supermarket and try to park its seven point five metre length among the other vehicles on a normal day. He wisely came with us!

But if ever there was a lady, this van was it. Far from being a monster as we had feared, it slid into all the spaces I tried, neatly and without fuss; and returning, I parked it between two others of its ilk, reversing in lengthwise with no problem; both we and the salesman being relieved we went ahead and ordered one.

We collected it three months later. Overjoyed with our new acquisition we started off back to England, unregistered, and on the dealer's own temporary plates, so we were chaperoned to the ferry by one of his men, who collected their property on arrival, wished us luck and vanished. Getting onto the ferry was interesting, and it was with considerable relief that we were able to get aboard safely.

Arriving back in England we had to site the van near Dover and wait there while the paperwork was done, duty paid, and proper plates made up. All at once, again, we were free, and the only barrier was the English Channel…

One small incident amused us during this time. Parked on the campsite we were sitting having tea one afternoon when a small family walked past, the young son eyeing our luxury with distaste, and we heard his comment to his parents as they passed by, which was "Who do they think they are!"

Well…..'We' certainly didn't know the answer!

The dogs had been cared for in a home near Calais, it was meant to have been a kennel but the owners could not bear to cage their guests, and so the house was nearly always rampant with dogs including their own much loved Labrador, 'Bertie'.

Ours fitted in as if they had always been part of the extended family and for this we were most grateful. Not that it was exceptional, we had also enjoyed the time when we put them with a Dutch lady near Perigueux. We had arrived to find the gate shut firmly but our ring on the dangling bell brought a small procession to meet us. In the lead was a small terrier, followed by a Sealyham, two greyhounds, a collie, and a wolfhound and deerhound loping across the grass towards us. Their guardian, a large and smiling woman let us in and escorted us to the house. I had a large deer-hound holding me carefully by the wrist and I didn't argue, he could have led me to heaven before I was going to object! Jan was escorted by the greyhounds and terrier, and we were ushered indoors.

Here a most extraordinary scene met our gaze. The sitting room was big and scattered around it were several large leather covered chairs, with 'numnahs' thrown over them as covers; each chair had an occupant: a large or small dog, there was another deer-hound an Airedale, a couple of Wymaras and another Labrador, a terrier gambolled at our feet and a beagle stretched her length across the fireplace while from outside a donkey with overgrown hooves clattered in; clearly animals here were the owners!

Our pampered hounds spent a very happy month there, and now it was good to find Sandy and Vera prepared to do the same. They became part of our lives; whenever we had need to shuttle to and from England, behind their home were wide fields and copses, and they would take all the dogs for long walks a couple of times a day through this heaven; certainly our two never objected to being with them, and often we had a job to prise them away.

Indeed it was rather like the friends in Pembrokeshire who had cared for them once. We had returned from our perambulations to find Lucy, the elder of the two, ensconced in a chair on the patio in the sun and little Judy missing; we made enquiry. "Oh she'll be over at the farm watching the new calf being born" we were told, Sure enough, in she came, a streak of dung across her nose; ignoring us with disdain she headed for the snack bar...

It was always good to be able to find our girls cared for, and now, reunited we could look forward to some travelling life in our large new home on wheels.

But first we had to return to the agent we had bought the van from for some added extras we had chosen which had not been in stock at the time we collected the van.

This was annoying, it was one of the hottest weeks on record, there was no shade in the agent's yard so along with another English van we sweated and cursed, but we were in a line and there were people before us; there was nothing to do but 'birsle' as the Scots say.

Our turn did come after two days of this misery. Unable even to plug in to mains due to a power cut we dripped distress and venom. We wanted a roof-rack fitting together with extra sockets over the table area, and after a noisy and dusty day eventually got them and could at last leave for our French home and hopefully find some shade on the way.

I have told the story of that trip before, but to recount, we ran right into a French Transport strike. Fuel was one of the first things hit, we had not thought it necessary to fill up in Belgium and all at once getting back home was going to be a very close run thing on the half-tank we already had.

We made it, thanks to pussyfoot-driving and finding a garage near Auxerre, run by a dear lady who allowed us twenty litres in a can, and a trickle from her pumps, but we reached home with the gauge firmly on zero.

It was interesting to discover as we tried to park, that the new van was actually longer than our little house; hurried stony additions to the parking area made a large enough stance, and except for the nerve wracking drive from the main road up to the cottage – little wider than the van and with many blind corners – it was amazing that over the course of the next two years we only met a tractor once, a nose to nose encounter that had us both cringing for a gateway to pass in.

The local farmer was very good, suggesting only that we blew hard on the horn in future so he would have some warning of our presence. Turning a large tractor with a 'gang' plough on the back is almost as hard as backing a twenty-five foot motor home down a ten foot wide winding track, as we both agreed!

Living as we did, half the year in our French doll's-house on the hill, half in the motor home, we had an enviable life, our boating days had given us rich memories and these corners were being reinforced and expanded with every season as we

144

discovered yet more of the richness of the land we called home.

Small journeys became extended forays, sometimes dramatic, as when Jan managed to break her ankle near La Rochelle. Even with the big van we discovered that moving around could be daunting, going to the loo impossible in the ordinary way. As in our old boating days poor Jan ended up having to use a bucket wedged between the settees and where she could reach a post to haul herself upright again. For the next three weeks she had to be still and the local district nurse came to give her injections against pleurisy, all of them in her poor tum!

Life goes on changing. Eventually we are all faced with life altering decisions. We could not contemplate retirement in France, becoming elderly or ill is best done in one's own language. A new corner has been looked around, a new chapter is being written, we can look back with thankfulness and joy at lives filled with scenes, places, peoples and experiences, our hearts still rejoicing and dreams still lying in wait round the next corner... or the next.

Postscript

We are often asked which memories have struck deepest in us.

One such must be that of our visit to Oradour sur Glane, the scene of one of those inexplicable events when mankind seems to lose every vestige of its humanity and commits acts outside expectation.

To go there is to be an unwilling part of the events which took place in a normal small town in France on a day during the latter part of the Second World War.

Ghosts abound; the town has been left as it was at the end of that afternoon, largely tumbled ruins – but nothing else has been touched – time has only slightly softened the ruins and only slightly healed memories, today we see the same acts still being repeated around our world.

To walk Oradour's streets is to be made eerily aware of what can happen suddenly to ordinary people on an ordinary day. No one has ever properly explained why these events took place, some say one thing, some another. Perhaps the truth will always remain buried along with anyone who might have been able to explain.

Imagine then, a town going about its business, in the local garage the owner/mechanic delves beneath a jacked-up car.

Along the street the seamstress works away at her sewing machine, in the Post Office people wait to buy stamps or make phone calls. The people who work in a nearby city have caught their bus and gone to their businesses, in the church flowers are being arranged in readiness for Mass or Sunday's services, farm workers labour in the fields, nothing is out of the ordinary. A couple of elderly men have gone off to fish in the river.

Into this peace a division of 2nd Panzers known as 'Das Reich' suddenly arrive. They quickly spread out across the town; the 180 soldiers order townsfolk to assemble in the marketplace for a 'security' check. They round up those working out in the fields and put them with the others. All are then divided into groups: men taken to nearby barns, women and children to the church. At four o'clock there is the sound of an explosion; SS troops suddenly open fire on their hostages, killing all the men and covering the bodies with hay and wood before burning them.

They also opened fire on the women and children in the church killing most of them, about two hundred people were there and it too was set on fire, only one person escaped. The town itself was destroyed.

In all six hundred and forty-two people were murdered that afternoon and even now nobody really knows why. It is said that the French Resistance had been very active in the region and that the explosion was some of their work, the town and its inhabitants may have been punished because of that.

The Allied invasion had just begun, Normandy had been invaded, the Germans were jumpy and unpredictable at that time.

Once again we find ourselves bemused at the unpredictable nature of man, that from a peaceful day could come such unbelievable callousness. One can only imagine how one would feel to be suddenly – in the midst of one's daily round – ordered from one's home or workplace, rounded up and a few hours later killed, without chance of protest or refusal.

It can happen, it does happen, even now. As always we are left with the question 'Why, why, why, why? But silence enfolds the ruins of Oradour and returns no answers....

Another moving experience was a visit to the War cemetery at Thiepval. Here a vast arched monument sits upon columns of marble, these carved with some seventy-two thousand names. These are the 'Missing' whose bodies were never found and who have no known grave.

In the turmoil of war thousands can vanish, lost in shell holes, caught in ambush, blown to pieces, unrecorded save from the files which once bore their names.

Thiepval breaks your heart. No matter how prepared you may be, the sheer scale dwarfs you, your mind refusing to accept what the names and crosses are telling you, that this many men simply disappeared, unknown and unsung. It doesn't matter what nationality they were, ours or theirs, the pain is the same, somewhere families have mourned without any remains to bring a closure.

This is the toll of war, this the price of victory, these the tears of defeat and loss. Standing there, walking among the graves, reading from the book kept here for visitors to say what they wish, one is empty, hollow, unrequited, for at the end of the day there has been nothing to say...

Finding peace, space, room to grow in oneself, this has been one of the most memorable things about looking round the next corner, there are still many places where such peace can be found, where a reunion with ourselves and the divine is not only possible, but where we can consciously go to realise it.

Our world is getting smaller, our ability to travel widely, the arising in other nations of large groups of people who are now free to travel, discover, occupy and yearn for the more remote places on earth, has meant that there is less opportunity to find true solitude.

Yet humanity stands in need of such places as much now as it has ever done, and a growing understanding is evident that others think the same, and are beginning to realise the need to preserve them. We have known about species under threat for many years, people are starting to apply the same criteria to our Earth and above all, to ourselves.

Many of my treasured memories revolve around keeping that sense of peace, of unity with our Earth, and the richness such contacts can bring us if only we are willing to individually respect and sustain them.

Each of us is on a journey, what footprint shall we leave on this planet? or is it better that we leave no footprint at all...

Now and again we have found someone waiting round a corner, who has made a vast difference in our lives. At times these encounters may be brief, but their effects are never forgotten. One such was Gino Gianelli.

We were in La Spezia, driven to take shelter there by bad

weather as we made our way up the Italian coast from Naples heading for Genoa.

Crisis loomed, the yacht needed refuelling ere we could go on; we were short of money and as if to add to our troubles, the pound sterling began floating. The banks suddenly refused to accept any sterling, and as the owners had just sent us a cheque and the banks refused to process it, it meant that all at once we became semi-destitute until the situation improved.

Harbour dues were costly and were building up and to lessen them we chose to anchor 'off' coming ashore by dinghy when we needed to do so.

There was much sympathy around the port, but rules were rules and we were causing problems to the authorities who reminded us of it sadly but firmly at intervals.

By now we were living on rice and a few sardines, and were nearly out of those, things were getting tough. Into this impasse came Gino.

We had seen him daily, for he took a walk along the quay every morning, an elderly figure in a heavy black overcoat, hands clasped behind his back. He always gave us "Good morning" as he passed.

On this morning he waited for us as we came ashore, and asked very politely if he might come and see the yacht, saying he had been an engineer in the Italian navy when young and missed ships and the sea.

Naturally we were glad to take him aboard, where he sat with us after a trip round the boat, discussed our engine problems and had tea. We apologised that we had no biscuits nor food to offer him and he made sympathetic noises before asking to be taken ashore again.

Next morning he was there again, this time he had a shopping bag with him, and presented it to us. It was full of oranges, biscuits, some tinned steak, soups, indeed, to us at the time, a wealth of goodies!

We protested, but he waved it aside. "You will come with me to lunch tomorrow" he said. "I will fetch you in my car and we will go along the coast to a place I know."

He was as good as his word; next morning a car pulled up

exactly on time beside the landing stage, and Gino smilingly ushered us aboard.

We set off on a most beautiful if slightly hair-raising journey.

The road wound its way northward along the cliffs. Gino's sight was evidently failing and we had a nervous drive, but at length we reached the restaurant perched high above the misty blue sea.

Nothing was too much. The place was run by an old friend of Gino's, an ex-engineer like himself, and we were feted accordingly.

Every day thereafter Gino came aboard and had his tea with us, bringing us gifts of food, sardines, pastas, great chunks of fresh fish, prawns; we lived like kings, and this dear man would take nothing in return saying that he liked the English, and was proud to be of service to us.

When we had to leave we were all tearful, we knew that probably we should never meet again, but a bond had been formed which tore at our heartstrings as we all said our goodbyes. Gino, I know you will have long gone to your rest, but two very grateful people bless you, and have never forgotten you. "Ciao mio Amigo…."

There have been others, people who touched us with their kindness and generosity of spirit, people who give the lie to the brief darkness of places like Oradour.

We lay for a few days once, in Santa Pola near Alicante. We were taking a large and decrepit motor yacht back to the UK, and the weather was in one of its habitual sulky periods; the yacht was scarcely seaworthy and we judged it better to remain where we were until calmer conditions came along.

Short of money again – another hiccup in the financial system – we were living close to the knuckle.

We had moored at a stretch of quay near the end of the port, and here, as evening came, we were joined by the fishing fleet. These were not the modern sleek vessels found in wealthier places; no, here they were of that older type, high bowed, flimsy wheelhouse, open deck, and a thudding great engine.

We discovered this as the first slid alongside and tied up to us; at once the yacht began to vibrate. The big semi-diesels of these fishing craft went round slowly, boomp, boomp, boomp! and our whole craft down to the last rivet and candelabra shuddered in sympathy!

The crews had complete faith in these monstrous machines, but it meant that every morning we would be woken at about four o'clock by the first of them starting up, followed over an hour, by all the rest. There was nothing to be done, their crews understood, as they came back in the evening, they would leave us small boxes of fishlets, often depriving themselves, for their catches were not large in any case; but they did this from their good simple hearts, sharing what they had with us strangers even though we had far more than they, yet wishing us well as we ate.

We sat often on the quayside with them sharing their meals under the stars: grilled sardines, slabs of fish from their catches, each boat contributing, we were never left out while we were among them, those are the kind of people we will never forget....ever.

Corners remain, there are not so many now, but we learned much, experienced many things. The saying that we gleaned from sailing friends years back which has been our own watchword is still as apposite today as it was then. "Take a chance and you'll never be sorry for a 'might have been'"

The years have passed, as has the companion of these travels, yet somehow I can still sense her joy as we planned or contemplated some new adventure. Things change, but 'The next corner' always awaits the curious soul... We always looked round ours; why not take a look around yours? You may be astonished at what you find!